D0520774

Houghton
Mifflin
Harcourt

CALIFORNIA
MATH
Expressions
Common Core

Dr. Karen C. Fuson

GRADE

3

Volume 1

This material is based upon work supported by the
National Science Foundation
under Grant Numbers
ESI-9816320, REC-9806020, and RED-935373.

Any opinions, findings, and conclusions, or recommendations expressed in this material
are those of the author and do not necessarily reflect the views of the National Science Foundation.

Name _____   **Date** _____

Use this chart to practice your 5s count-bys and multiplications. Then have your Homework Helper test you.

5s	In Order	Mixed Up
	$1 \times 5 = 5$	$9 \times 5 = 45$
	$2 \times 5 = 10$	$5 \times 5 = 25$
	$3 \times 5 = 15$	$2 \times 5 = 10$
	$4 \times 5 = 20$	$7 \times 5 = 35$
	$5 \times 5 = 25$	$4 \times 5 = 20$
	$6 \times 5 = 30$	$6 \times 5 = 30$
	$7 \times 5 = 35$	$10 \times 5 = 50$
	$8 \times 5 = 40$	$8 \times 5 = 40$
	$9 \times 5 = 45$	$1 \times 5 = 5$
	$10 \times 5 = 50$	$3 \times 5 = 15$

Homework

Name EMILY **Date** 1/3/23

Solve each equation. Then check your answers at the bottom of this page.

1. $8 \times 5 = \boxed{40}$ **2.** $9 \cdot 5 = \boxed{45}$ **3.** $5 * 2 = \boxed{10}$

4. $6 \times 5 = \boxed{30}$ **5.** $3 \cdot 5 = \boxed{15}$ **6.** $5 \times 4 = \boxed{20}$

7. $10 \times 5 = \boxed{50}$ **8.** $5 * 1 = \boxed{5}$ **9.** $6 \times 5 = \boxed{30}$

10. $5 * 5 = \boxed{}$ **11.** $5 \cdot 7 = \boxed{}$ **12.** $2 * 5 = \boxed{}$

13. $5 * 1 = \boxed{2}$ **14.** $5 \times 10 = \boxed{}$ **15.** $4 \cdot 5 = \boxed{}$

16. $7 \cdot 5 = \boxed{}$ **17.** $5 \times 2 = \boxed{}$ **18.** $5 * 7 = \boxed{}$

19. $5 \times 5 = \boxed{}$ **20.** $5 * 8 = \boxed{}$ **21.** $9 \cdot 5 = \boxed{}$

1. 40 **2.** 45 **3.** 10 **4.** 30 **5.** 15 **6.** 20 **7.** 50 **8.** 5 **9.** 30 **10.** 25
11. 35 **12.** 10 **13.** 5 **14.** 50 **15.** 20 **16.** 35 **17.** 10 **18.** 35 **19.** 25
20. 40 **21.** 45

Multiply with 5

Name _____ **Date** _____

Homework

┌───┐
│ **Study Plan**   │
│   │
│   _____ │
│   Homework Helper   │
└───┘

Write each total.

1. $2 \times ⑤ = 5 + 5 =$ _____

2. $4 \bullet ⑤ = 5 + 5 + 5 + 5 =$ _____

3. $6 * ⑤ = 5 + 5 + 5 + 5 + 5 + 5 =$ _____

Write the 5s additions that show each multiplication.
Then write the total.

4. $3 \times ⑤ =$ _____ $=$ _____

5. $5 * ⑤ =$ _____ $=$ _____

6. $1 \bullet ⑤ =$ _____ $=$ _____

7. $8 \bullet ⑤ =$ _____ $=$ _____

8. $7 \times ⑤ =$ _____ $=$ _____

Remembering

Count by 5s to find the total number.

  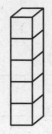 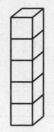 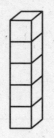 

1. 5   _____ 10   _____ 15   _____ 20   _____ 25

2. 65   _____   _____   15   _____   25

3. 30   20   35   40   45   50

4. 45   55   60   65   70   75

5. 75   80   85   90   95   100

6. **Stretch Your Thinking** Liam starts at a number and counts by 5s. He counts by 5s six times and is now at the number 75. What number did Liam start counting from? Explain how you know.

He started at 45

_____

_____

_____

_____

Homework

Name Emily   **Date** 12/29/22

Study Plan

Homework Helper

Write a multiplication equation to find the total number.

1. How many apples?

6   12   18   24

2. How many lenses?

2   4   6   10   14   14

Make a math drawing and label it with a multiplication equation. Then write the answer to the problem.

3. Beth put the dinner rolls she baked in 5 bags, with 6 rolls per bag. How many rolls did Beth bake?

5×6=30

30 rolls

4. Baya arranged her pennies into 7 piles of 5. How many pennies did she have?

7×5=35

75×

35

Remembering

Write each total.

1. $3 \times \boxed{5} = 5 + 5 + 5 =$ ___15___

2. $5 \bullet \boxed{5} = 5 + 5 + 5 + 5 + 5 =$ ___25___

Write the 5s additions that show each multiplication.
Then write the total.

3. $4 * \boxed{5} =$ ___5 + 5 + 5 + 5___ $=$ ___20___

4. $6 \times \boxed{5} =$ ___5 + 5 + 5 + 5 + 5 + 5___ $=$ ___30___

Write each product.

5. $7 \times 5 =$ ___35___   **6.** $9 * 5 =$ ___45___   **7.** $8 \bullet 5 =$ ___40___

8. $10 * 5 =$ ___50___   **9.** $1 \bullet 5 =$ ___5___   **10.** $5 \times 2 =$ ___10___

11. $5 \bullet 3 =$ ___15___   **12.** $5 * 4 =$ ___20___   **13.** $5 \times 5 =$ ___25___

14. Stretch Your Thinking Draw a picture to
show 3×5. Explain your drawing, and
find the product.

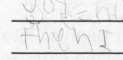

_____
_____
_____
_____

Multiplication as Equal Groups

Homework

Name _____   Date _____

Home Study Sheet A

5s

Count-bys	Mixed Up ×	Mixed Up ÷
1 × 5 = 5	2 × 5 = 10	10 ÷ 5 = 2
2 × 5 = 10	9 × 5 = 45	35 ÷ 5 = 7
3 × 5 = 15	1 × 5 = 5	50 ÷ 5 = 10
4 × 5 = 20	5 × 5 = 25	5 ÷ 5 = 1
5 × 5 = 25	7 × 5 = 35	20 ÷ 5 = 4
6 × 5 = 30	3 × 5 = 15	15 ÷ 5 = 3
7 × 5 = 35	10 × 5 = 50	30 ÷ 5 = 6
8 × 5 = 40	6 × 5 = 30	40 ÷ 5 = 8
9 × 5 = 45	4 × 5 = 20	25 ÷ 5 = 5
10 × 5 = 50	8 × 5 = 40	45 ÷ 5 = 9

2s

Count-bys	Mixed Up ×	Mixed Up ÷
1 × 2 = 2	7 × 2 = 14	20 ÷ 2 = 10
2 × 2 = 4	1 × 2 = 2	2 ÷ 2 = 1
3 × 2 = 6	3 × 2 = 6	6 ÷ 2 = 3
4 × 2 = 8	5 × 2 = 10	16 ÷ 2 = 8
5 × 2 = 10	6 × 2 = 12	12 ÷ 2 = 6
6 × 2 = 12	8 × 2 = 16	4 ÷ 2 = 2
7 × 2 = 14	2 × 2 = 4	10 ÷ 2 = 5
8 × 2 = 16	10 × 2 = 20	8 ÷ 2 = 4
9 × 2 = 18	4 × 2 = 8	14 ÷ 2 = 7
10 × 2 = 20	9 × 2 = 18	18 ÷ 2 = 9

10s

Count-bys	Mixed Up ×	Mixed Up ÷
1 × 10 = 10	1 × 10 = 10	80 ÷ 10 = 8
2 × 10 = 20	5 × 10 = 50	10 ÷ 10 = 1
3 × 10 = 30	2 × 10 = 20	50 ÷ 10 = 5
4 × 10 = 40	8 × 10 = 80	90 ÷ 10 = 9
5 × 10 = 50	7 × 10 = 70	40 ÷ 10 = 4
6 × 10 = 60	3 × 10 = 30	100 ÷ 10 = 10
7 × 10 = 70	4 × 10 = 40	30 ÷ 10 = 3
8 × 10 = 80	6 × 10 = 60	20 ÷ 10 = 2
9 × 10 = 90	10 × 10 = 100	70 ÷ 10 = 7
10 × 10 = 100	9 × 10 = 90	60 ÷ 10 = 6

9s

Count-bys	Mixed Up ×	Mixed Up ÷
1 × 9 = 9	2 × 9 = 18	81 ÷ 9 = 9
2 × 9 = 18	4 × 9 = 36	18 ÷ 9 = 2
3 × 9 = 27	7 × 9 = 63	36 ÷ 9 = 4
4 × 9 = 36	8 × 9 = 72	9 ÷ 9 = 1
5 × 9 = 45	3 × 9 = 27	54 ÷ 9 = 6
6 × 9 = 54	10 × 9 = 90	27 ÷ 9 = 3
7 × 9 = 63	1 × 9 = 9	63 ÷ 9 = 7
8 × 9 = 72	6 × 9 = 54	72 ÷ 9 = 8
9 × 9 = 81	5 × 9 = 45	90 ÷ 9 = 10
10 × 9 = 90	9 × 9 = 81	45 ÷ 9 = 5

Homework

Home Signature Sheet

	Count-Bys Homework Helper	Multiplications Homework Helper	Divisions Homework Helper
0			
1			
2			
3			
4			
5			
6			
7			
8			
9			
10			

Homework

Name _____ **Date** _____

Study Plan

_____
Homework Helper

Write a multiplication equation for each array.

1. How many muffins?

$3 \times 4 = 12$

_____

2. How many basketballs?

$5 \times 6 = 30$

_____

Make a math drawing for each problem and label it with a multiplication equation. Then write the answer to the problem.

3. Ellie arranged her trophies in 3 rows, with 6 trophies in each row. How many trophies does she have?

_____

4. Maribel planted a garden with 9 tomato plants in each of 2 rows. How many tomato plants did she plant?

_____

Name _____ Date _____

Remembering

Write each product.

1. 1 * 5 = ☐

2. 8 • 5 = ☐

3. 5 × 2 = ☐

4. 9 × 5 = ☐

5. 10 * 5 = ☐

6. 4 • 5 = ☐

Write a multiplication equation to find the total number.

7. How many cubes?

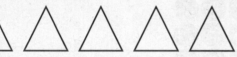

_____

8. How many sides?

_____

9. How many sides?

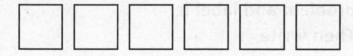

_____

10. Stretch Your Thinking Miles has 24 baseball cards.
He wants to display the cards in even rows and
columns. Draw two different arrays to show how
Miles could display his cards. Label your drawings
with a multiplication equation.

_____ _____

Homework

Use this chart to practice your 5s count-bys, multiplications, and divisions. Then have your Homework Helper test you.

In Order ×	Mixed Up ×	Mixed Up ÷
1 × 5 = 5	4 × 5 = 20	20 ÷ 5 = 4
2 × 5 = 10	7 × 5 = 35	5 ÷ 5 = 1
3 × 5 = 15	2 × 5 = 10	50 ÷ 5 = 10
4 × 5 = 20	5 × 5 = 25	35 ÷ 5 = 7
5 × 5 = 25	9 × 5 = 45	15 ÷ 5 = 3
6 × 5 = 30	1 × 5 = 5	45 ÷ 5 = 9
7 × 5 = 35	10 × 5 = 50	10 ÷ 5 = 2
8 × 5 = 40	3 × 5 = 15	25 ÷ 5 = 5
9 × 5 = 45	6 × 5 = 30	40 ÷ 5 = 8
10 × 5 = 50	8 × 5 = 40	30 ÷ 5 = 6

5s

Homework

**Multiply or divide to find the unknown numbers.
Then check your answers at the bottom of this page.**

1. $5 \times 6 = \boxed{}$

2. $45 \div 5 = \boxed{}$

3. $5 \times \boxed{} = 35$

4. $\boxed{} \times 5 = 10$

5. $3 \times 5 = \boxed{}$

6. $50 / 5 = \boxed{}$

7. $5 \bullet 9 = \boxed{}$

8. $\boxed{} \bullet 5 = 20$

9. $5\overline{)25}$

10. $5 * \boxed{} = 40$

11. $5 \bullet 5 = \boxed{}$

12. $\frac{35}{5} = \boxed{}$

13. $5 \bullet \boxed{} = 15$

14. $30 \div 5 = \boxed{}$

15. $5 \times \boxed{} = 45$

16. $\boxed{} \div 5 = 7$

17. $\frac{10}{5} = \boxed{}$

18. $5 \bullet 8 = \boxed{}$

19. $5\overline{)20}$

20. $5 \times \boxed{} = 5$

21. $5 \times \boxed{} = 50$

1. 30 **2.** 9 **3.** 7 **4.** 2 **5.** 15 **6.** 10 **7.** 45 **8.** 4 **9.** 5 **10.** 8 **11.** 25
12. 7 **13.** 3 **14.** 6 **15.** 9 **16.** 35 **17.** 2 **18.** 40 **19.** 4 **20.** 1 **21.** 10

Homework

Study Plan

Homework Helper

Write a multiplication equation and a division equation for each problem. Then solve the problem.

1. Mandy's Diner has a total of 20 chairs. The chairs are divided equally among 5 tables. How many chairs are at each table?

   Show your work.

2. Tarek divided 30 nickels into 5 piles. He put the same number of nickels in each pile. How many nickels were in each pile?

3. A group of singers has 45 members. The singers are arranged in groups of 5 on the stage. How many groups are there?

4. Brianna arranged 40 marbles into an array with 5 marbles in each row. How many rows of marbles were in her array?

Remembering

Make a math drawing for the problem and label it with a multiplication equation. Then write the answer to the problem.

1. Ann has 5 boxes with 7 crayons in each box. How many crayons does Ann have?

2. Mr. Garcia displays the school trophies in 3 rows of 5. How many trophies does Mr. Garcia display?

_____

_____

Write a multiplication equation for each array.

3. How many dots?

_____

4. How many cubes?

_____

5. **Stretch Your Thinking** Write a real world division problem using 5 as the divisor. Then solve your problem.

_____

_____

_____

The Meaning of Division

Use this chart to practice your 2s count-bys, multiplications, and divisions. Then have your Homework Helper test you.

	× In Order	× Mixed Up	÷ Mixed Up
2s	1 × 2 = 2	4 × 2 = 8	18 ÷ 2 = 9
	2 × 2 = 4	7 × 2 = 14	6 ÷ 2 = 3
	3 × 2 = 6	2 × 2 = 4	2 ÷ 2 = 1
	4 × 2 = 8	5 × 2 = 10	16 ÷ 2 = 8
	5 × 2 = 10	9 × 2 = 18	14 ÷ 2 = 7
	6 × 2 = 12	1 × 2 = 2	4 ÷ 2 = 2
	7 × 2 = 14	10 × 2 = 20	20 ÷ 2 = 10
	8 × 2 = 16	3 × 2 = 6	8 ÷ 2 = 4
	9 × 2 = 18	6 × 2 = 12	12 ÷ 2 = 6
	10 × 2 = 20	8 × 2 = 16	10 ÷ 2 = 5

Name _____ Date _____

Homework

Multiply or divide to find the unknown numbers. Then check your answers at the bottom of this page.

1. $2 \times 4 =$ ☐

2. $20 \div 5 =$ ☐

3. $6 * 2 =$ ☐

4. $45 / 5 =$ ☐

5. $2 \cdot 10 =$ ☐

6. $\frac{20}{2} =$ ☐

7. $5 \times 10 =$ ☐

8. $16 \div 2 =$ ☐

9. $6 \times 5 =$ ☐

10. $30 / 5 =$ ☐

11. $5 \cdot 7 =$ ☐

12. $2 \overline{)18}$

13. $8 * 2 =$ ☐

14. $\frac{25}{5} =$ ☐

15. $5 \cdot 4 =$ ☐

16. $16 / 2 =$ ☐

17. $2 \overline{)10}$

18. $2 * 7 =$ ☐

19. $5 \times 5 =$ ☐

20. $14 \div 2 =$ ☐

21. $\frac{☐}{5} = 7$

1. 8 2. 4 3. 12 4. 9 5. 20 6. 10 7. 50 8. 8 9. 30 10. 6 11. 35 12. 9 13. 16 14. 5 15. 20 16. 8 17. 5 18. 14 19. 25 20. 7 21. 35

Multiply and Divide with 2

Homework

Home Check Sheet 1: 5s and 2s

5s Multiplication	5s Divisions	2s Multiplications	2s Divisions
$2 \times 5 = 10$	$30 / 5 = 6$	$4 \times 2 = 8$	$8 / 2 = 4$
$5 \cdot 6 = 30$	$5 \div 5 = 1$	$2 \cdot 8 = 16$	$18 \div 2 = 9$
$5 * 9 = 45$	$15 / 5 = 3$	$1 * 2 = 2$	$2 / 2 = 1$
$4 \times 5 = 20$	$50 \div 5 = 10$	$6 \times 2 = 12$	$16 \div 2 = 8$
$5 \cdot 7 = 35$	$20 / 5 = 4$	$2 \cdot 9 = 18$	$4 / 2 = 2$
$10 * 5 = 50$	$10 \div 5 = 2$	$2 * 2 = 4$	$20 \div 2 = 10$
$1 \times 5 = 5$	$35 / 5 = 7$	$3 \times 2 = 6$	$10 / 2 = 5$
$5 \cdot 3 = 15$	$40 \div 5 = 8$	$2 \cdot 5 = 10$	$12 \div 2 = 6$
$8 * 5 = 40$	$25 / 5 = 5$	$10 * 2 = 20$	$6 / 2 = 3$
$5 \times 5 = 25$	$45 / 5 = 9$	$2 \times 7 = 14$	$14 / 2 = 7$
$5 \cdot 8 = 40$	$20 \div 5 = 4$	$2 \cdot 10 = 20$	$4 \div 2 = 2$
$7 * 5 = 35$	$15 / 5 = 3$	$9 * 2 = 18$	$2 / 2 = 1$
$5 \times 4 = 20$	$30 \div 5 = 6$	$2 \times 6 = 12$	$8 \div 2 = 4$
$6 \cdot 5 = 30$	$25 / 5 = 5$	$8 \cdot 2 = 16$	$6 / 2 = 3$
$5 * 1 = 5$	$10 \div 5 = 2$	$2 * 3 = 6$	$20 \div 2 = 10$
$5 \times 10 = 50$	$45 / 5 = 9$	$2 \times 2 = 4$	$14 / 2 = 7$
$9 \cdot 5 = 45$	$35 \div 5 = 7$	$1 \cdot 2 = 2$	$10 \div 2 = 5$
$5 * 2 = 10$	$50 \div 5 = 10$	$2 * 4 = 8$	$16 \div 2 = 8$
$3 \times 5 = 15$	$40 / 5 = 8$	$5 \times 2 = 10$	$12 / 2 = 6$
$5 \cdot 5 = 25$	$5 \div 5 = 1$	$7 \cdot 2 = 14$	$18 \div 2 = 9$

Homework

Study Plan

_____

Homework Helper

Write an equation and solve the problem.

1. Tanya had 14 cups to fill with juice. She put them in 2 equal rows. How many cups were in each row?

_____

2. Rebecca has 3 pairs of running shoes. She bought new shoelaces for each pair. How many shoelaces did she buy?

_____

3. Jason served his family dinner. He put 5 carrots on each of the 4 plates. How many carrots did Jason serve in all?

_____

4. Olivia filled 8 vases with flowers. She put 5 flowers in each vase. How many flowers did she put in the vases?

_____

5. Devon has 30 model airplanes. He put the same number on each of the 5 shelves of his bookcase. How many model airplanes did Devon put on each shelf?

_____

6. There are 12 eggs in a carton. They are arranged in 2 rows with the same number of eggs in each row. How many eggs are in each row?

_____

Name _____   **Date** _____

Remembering

Make a math drawing for the problem and label it with a multiplication equation. Then write the answer to the problem.

1. Kishore has 4 stacks with 3 books in each stack. How many books are there in all?

   _____

2. Cindy had 6 envelopes. She put 2 stamps on each one. How many stamps did she use?

   _____

Write a multiplication equation for the array.

3. How many dots?

   • • • • •
   • • • • •
   • • • • •   _____

Multiply or divide to find the unknown numbers.

4. $7 * 5 = \boxed{}$

5. $45 \div 5 = \boxed{}$

6. $\boxed{} \times 5 = 50$

7. $8 * 5 = \boxed{}$

8. $5 \cdot \boxed{} = 25$

9. $\dfrac{10}{5} = \boxed{}$

10. **Stretch Your Thinking** Explain how to solve the following problem using division and multiplication. There are 18 students in the classroom. There are 2 students in each group. How many groups of students are there?

   _____

   _____

Multiply and Divide with 2

Homework

Study Plan

Homework Helper

Write an equation and solve the problem.

1. On a wall, photos are arranged in 2 rows with 7 photos in each row. How many photos are on the wall?

_____

2. An orchard has 6 rows of apple trees. Each row has 5 trees. How many apple trees are in the orchard?

_____

3. Navin arranged his soccer trophies into 5 equal rows. He has 25 trophies. How many are in each row?

_____

4. Tickets to the school play cost $2 each. Mrs. Cortez spent $16 on tickets. How many tickets did she buy?

_____

5. Jimet solved 20 multiplications. There were 5 multiplications in each row. How many rows of multiplications did she solve?

_____

6. Josh has 2 peaches for each of his 6 friends. How many peaches does he have?

_____

Remembering

Write a multiplication equation for each array.

1. How many dots?

_____

2. How many dots?

_____

Multiply or divide to find the unknown numbers.

3. $2 \times 7 = \boxed{}$

4. $5 \cdot \boxed{} = 30$

5. $5)\overline{5}$

6. $25 \div 5 = \boxed{}$

7. $4 * 5 = \boxed{}$

8. $\frac{35}{5} = \boxed{}$

Write an equation and solve the problem.

9. There are 10 sunglasses on the display. Each has 2 lenses. How many lenses are there?

_____

_____

10. Bryce draws 40 stars on his poster. He draws 5 rows and puts the same number in each row. How many stars are in each row?

_____

_____

11. Stretch Your Thinking Sarah has 10 stuffed animals. Explain two different ways she can group the stuffed animals so each group has the same number and no stuffed animals are left over.

_____

_____

_____

Building Fluency with 2s and 5s

Use this chart to practice your 10s count-bys, multiplications, and divisions. Then have your Homework Helper test you.

	× In Order	× Mixed Up	÷ Mixed Up
10s	1 × 10 = 10	4 × 10 = 40	100 ÷ 10 = 10
	2 × 10 = 20	7 × 10 = 70	20 ÷ 10 = 2
	3 × 10 = 30	2 × 10 = 20	40 ÷ 10 = 4
	4 × 10 = 40	5 × 10 = 50	70 ÷ 10 = 7
	5 × 10 = 50	9 × 10 = 90	30 ÷ 10 = 3
	6 × 10 = 60	1 × 10 = 10	60 ÷ 10 = 6
	7 × 10 = 70	10 × 10 = 100	80 ÷ 10 = 8
	8 × 10 = 80	3 × 10 = 30	10 ÷ 10 = 1
	9 × 10 = 90	6 × 10 = 60	50 ÷ 10 = 5
	10 × 10 = 100	8 × 10 = 80	90 ÷ 10 = 9

Name   Date

Homework

Multiply or divide to find the unknown numbers. Then check your answers at the bottom of this page.

1. $2 \times 10 = \boxed{}$ **2.** $15 \div 5 = \boxed{}$ **3.** $4 * 2 = \boxed{}$

4. $80 / 10 = \boxed{}$ **5.** $5 \bullet \boxed{} = 40$ **6.** $\frac{60}{10} = \boxed{}$

7. $\boxed{} \times 5 = 30$ **8.** $\frac{20}{2} = \boxed{}$ **9.** $6 \times 10 = \boxed{}$

10. $25 / 5 = \boxed{}$ **11.** $10 \bullet 7 = \boxed{}$ **12.** $14 \div 2 = \boxed{}$

13. $9 * 2 = \boxed{}$ **14.** $\frac{45}{5} = \boxed{}$ **15.** $10 \bullet 4 = \boxed{}$

16. $2\overline{)20}$ (with box above)   **17.** $70 \div 10 = \boxed{}$ **18.** $9 * \boxed{} = 18$

19. $\boxed{} \times 5 = 35$ **20.** $\frac{\boxed{}}{3} = 10$ **21.** $\boxed{} \bullet 2 = 16$

1. 20 **2.** 3 **3.** 8 **4.** 8 **5.** 8 **6.** 6 **7.** 6 **8.** 10 **9.** 60 **10.** 5 **11.** 70 **12.** 7 **13.** 18 **14.** 9 **15.** 40 **16.** 10 **17.** 7 **18.** 2 **19.** 7 **20.** 30 **21.** 8

Homework

Study Plan
_____
Homework Helper

Write an equation and solve the problem.

1. Wendy has 100 cents. She wants to buy some marbles that cost 10 cents each. How many marbles can she buy?

   _____

2. Natalie turned off 2 lights in each of the 6 rooms of her house. How many lights did she turn off?

   _____

3. Luis has 18 single socks. How many pairs of socks does he have?

   _____

4. Lana has 9 nickels. She wants to buy an apple that costs 40 cents. Does she have enough money?

   _____

5. Annabelle had 20 crayons. She gave 5 of them to each of her sisters. How many sisters does Annabelle have?

   _____

6. Harvey wrote letters to 10 of his friends. Each letter was 3 pages long. How many pages did Harvey write?

   _____

Complete the table.

7.

Number of Nickels	1	3	5	8		
Total Amount		15¢			45¢	50¢

Name   **Date**

Remembering

Write a multiplication equation and a division equation for each problem. Then solve the problem.   *Show your work.*

1. Tara folds 25 sweaters. She puts the same number of sweaters in each pile. There are 5 piles. How many sweaters are in each pile?

   _____

2. Mr. McBride orders 30 new pencils. There are 5 pencils in each box. How many boxes of pencils does Mr. McBride order?

   _____

Multiply or divide to find the unknown numbers.

3. $5 \cdot \boxed{} = 45$ 4. $2\overline{)12}$ with $\boxed{}$ 5. $14 \div 2 = \boxed{}$

6. $\boxed{} * 5 = 20$ 7. $2 \times \boxed{} = 8$ 8. $\dfrac{16}{2} = \boxed{}$

Write an equation and solve the problem.

9. The books were put in 5 equal rows on display. There were 45 books. How many are in each row?

10. The class lined up in 2 rows with 8 students in each row. How many students are in the class?

   _____   _____

11. **Stretch Your Thinking** Explain how you know if a number can be divided by 10 evenly.

   _____

   _____

Homework

Use this chart to practice your 9s count-bys, multiplications, and divisions. Then have your Homework Helper test you.

9s	× In Order	× Mixed Up	÷ Mixed Up
	$1 \times 9 = 9$	$4 \times 9 = 36$	$63 \div 9 = 7$
	$2 \times 9 = 18$	$7 \times 9 = 63$	$9 \div 9 = 1$
	$3 \times 9 = 27$	$2 \times 9 = 18$	$54 \div 9 = 6$
	$4 \times 9 = 36$	$5 \times 9 = 45$	$18 \div 9 = 2$
	$5 \times 9 = 45$	$9 \times 9 = 81$	$90 \div 9 = 10$
	$6 \times 9 = 54$	$1 \times 9 = 9$	$81 \div 9 = 9$
	$7 \times 9 = 63$	$10 \times 9 = 90$	$45 \div 9 = 5$
	$8 \times 9 = 72$	$3 \times 9 = 27$	$27 \div 9 = 3$
	$9 \times 9 = 81$	$6 \times 9 = 54$	$36 \div 9 = 4$
	$10 \times 9 = 90$	$8 \times 9 = 72$	$72 \div 9 = 8$

Homework

Multiply or divide to find the unknown numbers. Then check your answers at the bottom of this page.

1. $2 \times 9 = \boxed{}$ **2.** $18 \div 2 = \boxed{}$ **3.** $6 * \boxed{} = 12$

4. $40 / 5 = \boxed{}$ **5.** $10 \cdot 8 = \boxed{}$ **6.** $\frac{27}{9} = \boxed{}$

7. $\boxed{} \times 5 = 40$ **8.** $2)\overline{14}$ with $\boxed{}$ above   **9.** $9 \times 10 = \boxed{}$

10. $\frac{60}{10} = \boxed{}$ **11.** $10 \cdot 7 = \boxed{}$ **12.** $72 \div 9 = \boxed{}$

13. $5 * 9 = \boxed{}$ **14.** $\frac{20}{2} = \boxed{}$ **15.** $9 \cdot \boxed{} = 36$

16. $10 / 2 = \boxed{}$ **17.** $63 \div 9 = \boxed{}$ **18.** $9 * 9 = \boxed{}$

19. $5 \times 5 = \boxed{}$ **20.** $5)\overline{30}$ with $\boxed{}$ above   **21.** $9 \times 3 = \boxed{}$

© Houghton Mifflin Harcourt Publishing Company

1. 18 **2.** 9 **3.** 2 **4.** 8 **5.** 80 **6.** 3 **7.** 8 **8.** 7 **9.** 90 **10.** 6 **11.** 70 **12.** 8 **13.** 45 **14.** 10 **15.** 4 **16.** 5 **17.** 7 **18.** 81 **19.** 25 **20.** 6 **21.** 27

Name _____ **Date** _____

Homework

Home Check Sheet 2: 10s and 9s

10s Multiplications	10s Divisions	9s Multiplications	9s Divisions
9 × 10 = 90	100 / 10 = 10	3 × 9 = 27	27 / 9 = 3
10 • 3 = 30	50 ÷ 10 = 5	9 • 7 = 63	9 ÷ 9 = 1
10 * 6 = 60	70 / 10 = 7	10 * 9 = 90	81 / 9 = 9
1 × 10 = 10	40 ÷ 10 = 4	5 × 9 = 45	45 ÷ 9 = 5
10 • 4 = 40	80 / 10 = 8	9 • 8 = 72	90 / 9 = 10
10 * 7 = 70	60 ÷ 10 = 6	9 * 1 = 9	36 ÷ 9 = 4
8 × 10 = 80	10 / 10 = 1	2 × 9 = 18	18 / 9 = 2
10 • 10 = 100	20 ÷ 10 = 2	9 • 9 = 81	63 ÷ 9 = 7
5 * 10 = 50	90 / 10 = 9	6 * 9 = 54	54 / 9 = 6
10 × 2 = 20	30 / 10 = 3	9 × 4 = 36	72 / 9 = 8
10 • 5 = 50	80 ÷ 10 = 8	9 • 5 = 45	27 ÷ 9 = 3
4 * 10 = 40	70 / 10 = 7	4 * 9 = 36	45 / 9 = 5
10 × 1 = 10	100 ÷ 10 = 10	9 × 1 = 9	63 ÷ 9 = 7
3 • 10 = 30	90 / 10 = 9	3 • 9 = 27	72 / 9 = 8
10 * 8 = 80	60 ÷ 10 = 6	9 * 8 = 72	54 ÷ 9 = 6
7 × 10 = 70	30 / 10 = 3	7 × 9 = 63	18 / 9 = 2
6 • 10 = 60	10 ÷ 10 = 1	6 • 9 = 54	90 ÷ 9 = 10
10 * 9 = 90	40 ÷ 10 = 4	9 * 9 = 81	9 ÷ 9 = 1
10 × 10 = 100	20 / 10 = 2	10 × 9 = 90	36 / 9 = 4
2 • 10 = 20	50 ÷ 10 = 5	2 • 9 = 18	81 ÷ 9 = 9

Homework

Study Plan
Homework Helper

Write an equation for each situation. Then solve the problem.

1. The pet store has 54 birds. There are 9 birds in each cage. How many cages are there?

   _____

2. George told 2 stories each night of the camping trip. The camping trip was 3 nights long. How many stories did George tell?

   _____

3. LaShawna blew up 40 balloons for a party. She made 10 equal bunches of balloons to put on the tables. How many balloons were in each bunch?

   _____

4. There are 4 floors in Redville City Hall. Every floor has 9 offices. How many offices are in the building?

   _____

5. Brigitte has 15 CDs. She can put 5 CDs in the CD player at one time. How many times does she have to change the CDs to listen to all of them?

   _____

Show your work.

Multiply and Divide with 9 **31**

Remembering

Multiply or divide to find the unknown numbers.

1. $\frac{40}{5} = \boxed{}$

2. $2 \times \boxed{} = 18$

3. $5 \bullet 5 = \boxed{}$

4. $15 \div 5 = \boxed{}$

5. $\boxed{} * 2 = 20$

6. $2\overline{)20}^{\boxed{}}$

Write an equation and solve the problem.

7. The parking lot has 45 cars. There are 5 cars in each row. How many rows of cars are there?

_____

8. A garden has 2 rows of tomato plants. Each row has 8 tomato plants. How many tomato plants are in the garden?

_____

9. The museum has 20 plaques hanging on the wall. The plaques are in 2 equal rows. How many plaques are in each row?

_____

10. Seven children each show 5 fingers. How many fingers are being shown?

_____

Complete the table.

11. Number of Dimes	1	3		7	9
Total Amount			50¢		90¢

12. **Stretch Your Thinking** The music teacher wants to line up the students to form an equal number of rows and columns for a performance. The music teacher wants 9 rows. Draw an array to show how the students will be lined up for the performance. How many students will there be?

Name _____ **Date** _____

Homework

Home Check Sheet 3: 2s, 5s, 9s, and 10s

2s, 5s, 9s,10s Multiplications	2s, 5s, 9s, 10s Multiplications	2s, 5s, 9s, 10s Divisions	2s, 5s, 9s, 10s Divisions
2 × 10 = 20	5 × 10 = 50	18 / 2 = 9	36 / 9 = 4
10 • 5 = 50	10 • 9 = 90	50 ÷ 5 = 10	70 ÷ 10 = 7
9 * 6 = 54	4 * 10 = 40	72 / 9 = 8	18 / 2 = 9
7 × 10 = 70	2 × 9 = 18	60 ÷ 10 = 6	45 ÷ 5 = 9
2 • 3 = 6	5 • 3 = 15	12 / 2 = 6	45 / 9 = 5
5 * 7 = 35	6 * 9 = 54	30 ÷ 5 = 6	30 ÷ 10 = 3
9 × 10 = 90	10 × 3 = 30	18 / 9 = 2	6 / 2 = 3
6 • 10 = 60	3 • 2 = 6	50 ÷ 10 = 5	50 ÷ 5 = 10
8 * 2 = 16	5 * 8 = 40	14 / 2 = 7	27 / 9 = 3
5 × 6 = 30	9 × 9 = 81	25 / 5 = 5	70 / 10 = 7
9 • 5 = 45	10 • 4 = 40	81 ÷ 9 = 9	20 ÷ 2 = 10
8 * 10 = 80	9 * 2 = 18	20 / 10 = 2	45 / 5 = 9
2 × 1 = 2	5 × 1 = 5	8 ÷ 2 = 4	54 ÷ 9 = 6
3 • 5 = 15	9 • 6 = 54	45 / 5 = 9	80 / 10 = 8
4 * 9 = 36	10 * 1 = 10	63 ÷ 9 = 7	16 ÷ 2 = 8
3 × 10 = 30	7 × 2 = 14	30 / 10 = 3	15 / 5 = 3
2 • 6 = 12	6 • 5 = 30	10 ÷ 2 = 5	90 ÷ 9 = 10
4 * 5 = 20	8 * 9 = 72	40 ÷ 5 = 8	100 ÷ 10 = 10
9 × 7 = 63	10 × 6 = 60	9 / 9 = 1	12 / 2 = 6
1 • 10 = 10	2 • 8 = 16	50 ÷ 10 = 5	35 ÷ 5 = 7

Homework

Multiply or divide to find the unknown numbers. Then check your answers at the bottom of this page.

1. $5 \times 6 = \boxed{}$

2. $50 \div 10 = \boxed{}$

3. $6 * 9 = \boxed{}$

4. $12 / 2 = \boxed{}$

5. $9 \times \boxed{} = 72$

6. $\frac{14}{2} = \boxed{}$

7. $9 \bullet 5 = \boxed{}$

8. $15 \div 5 = \boxed{}$

9. $7 \times 2 = \boxed{}$

10. $25 / 5 = \boxed{}$

11. $10 \bullet \boxed{} = 40$

12. $9 \overline{)27}$

13. $8 * 5 = \boxed{}$

14. $\frac{81}{9} = \boxed{}$

15. $7 \bullet \boxed{} = 35$

16. $2 \overline{)20}$

17. $10 \div \boxed{} = 5$

18. $2 * 7 = \boxed{}$

19. $30 \div 5 = \boxed{}$

20. $2 \times 7 = \boxed{}$

21. $18 / 2 = \boxed{}$

1. 30 **2.** 5 **3.** 54 **4.** 6 **5.** 8 **6.** 7 **7.** 45 **8.** 3 **9.** 14 **10.** 5 **11.** 4 **12.** 3 **13.** 40 **14.** 9 **15.** 5 **16.** 10 **17.** 2 **18.** 14 **19.** 6 **20.** 14 **21.** 9

Homework

Study Plan

Homework Helper

Write an equation for each situation. Then solve the problem.

1. Quinn rode his bike 35 miles. He stopped for water every 5 miles. How many times did Quinn stop for water?

_____

2. Roy had 12 bottles of juice. He put them in the refrigerator in 2 rows. How many bottles were in each row?

_____

3. Melinda has 5 cousins. She called each one on the phone 4 times this month. How many phone calls did she make to her cousins this month?

_____

4. Janelle won 27 tickets at the fair. She traded the tickets for 9 prizes. Each prize was worth the same number of tickets. How many tickets was each prize worth?

_____

5. Eric had 2 picnic baskets. He put 7 apples in each one. How many apples did he put into the picnic baskets?

_____

6. Grace has read 2 chapters in each of her 9 books. How many chapters has she read in all?

_____

Remembering

Write an equation and solve the problem.

1. Maria wants some pens that cost $2 each. She spends $12 on pens. How many pens does she buy?

   _____

2. Mrs. Lee has 5 crayons for each of her 10 students. How many crayons does Mrs. Lee have?

   _____

Multiply or divide to find the unknown numbers.

3. $5 \cdot 1 = \boxed{}$

4. $2 \times \boxed{} = 8$

5. $\dfrac{90}{10} = \boxed{}$

6. $30 \div 10 = \boxed{}$

7. $2\overline{)14}$

8. $\boxed{} * 5 = 35$

Write an equation and solve the problem.

9. The art teacher has 63 paintbrushes. There are 9 paintbrushes in each box. How many boxes are there?

   _____

10. There are 8 plates. Jamie puts 9 strawberries on each plate. How many strawberries are on the plates?

   _____

11. Mr. Kim receives an order of 30 new books for the media center. He displays the same number of books on each of 5 shelves. How many books are on each shelf?

   _____

12. **Stretch Your Thinking** Write a word problem using 9 and 10 as factors. Write an equation to solve your problem.

   _____

   _____

      Building Fluency with 2s, 5s, 9s, and 10s

Homework

Use this chart to practice your 3s count-bys, multiplications, and divisions. Then have your Homework Helper test you.

	× In Order	× Mixed Up	÷ Mixed Up
3s	$1 \times 3 = 3$	$3 \times 3 = 9$	$27 \div 3 = 9$
	$2 \times 3 = 6$	$5 \times 3 = 15$	$21 \div 3 = 7$
	$3 \times 3 = 9$	$1 \times 3 = 3$	$3 \div 3 = 1$
	$4 \times 3 = 12$	$8 \times 3 = 24$	$9 \div 3 = 3$
	$5 \times 3 = 15$	$2 \times 3 = 6$	$30 \div 3 = 10$
	$6 \times 3 = 18$	$9 \times 3 = 27$	$24 \div 3 = 8$
	$7 \times 3 = 21$	$7 \times 3 = 21$	$12 \div 3 = 4$
	$8 \times 3 = 24$	$10 \times 3 = 30$	$6 \div 3 = 2$
	$9 \times 3 = 27$	$6 \times 3 = 18$	$15 \div 3 = 5$
	$10 \times 3 = 30$	$4 \times 3 = 12$	$18 \div 3 = 6$

Name _____ **Date** _____

Homework

Multiply or divide to find the unknown numbers. Then check your answers at the bottom of this page.

1. $6 \times 3 = \boxed{}$

2. $3\overline{)27}$ with box above

3. $2 * \boxed{} = 18$

4. $18 / 9 = \boxed{}$

5. $3 \times \boxed{} = 30$

6. $\frac{15}{3} = \boxed{}$

7. $9 \cdot 8 = \boxed{}$

8. $50 \div 10 = \boxed{}$

9. $2 \times 2 = \boxed{}$

10. $35 / 5 = \boxed{}$

11. $4 \cdot 10 = \boxed{}$

12. $14 \div 2 = \boxed{}$

13. $8 * 3 = \boxed{}$

14. $\frac{63}{9} = \boxed{}$

15. $5 \cdot \boxed{} = 35$

16. $9\overline{)27}$ with box above

17. $10 \div \boxed{} = 2$

18. $\boxed{} * 9 = 18$

19. $5 \times 9 = \boxed{}$

20. $81 \div \boxed{} = 9$

21. $14 / 2 = \boxed{}$

1. 18 **2.** 9 **3.** 9 **4.** 2 **5.** 10 **6.** 5 **7.** 72 **8.** 5 **9.** 4 **10.** 7 **11.** 40
12. 7 **13.** 24 **14.** 7 **15.** 7 **16.** 3 **17.** 5 **18.** 2 **19.** 45 **20.** 9 **21.** 7

Multiply and Divide with 3

Name _____ Date _____

Write an equation and solve the problem.

1. Greg has 3 hats. He has worn each one 4 times this year. How many times this year has he worn a hat?

_____

2. Keenan has won 24 award ribbons. He hung them on his wall in 3 rows, with the same number of ribbons in each row. How many ribbons are in each row?

_____

3. Mai went to the movies 9 times this month. She paid 4 dollars to see each movie. How much did she spend in all?

_____

4. Tess planted 45 tomato seeds in her garden. She planted them in an array with 9 rows. How many seeds were in each row?

_____

Find the total number by starting with the fifth count-by and counting from there.

5. How many bananas are in these 9 bunches?

___ ___ ___ ___

Remembering

Multiply or divide to find the unknown numbers.

1. $2 \cdot 2 = \boxed{}$

2. $10 \times \boxed{} = 70$

3. $\dfrac{36}{9} = \boxed{}$

4. $\boxed{} * 9 = 72$

5. $20 \div 10 = \boxed{}$

6. $\boxed{} * 10 = 40$

Write an equation for each situation. Then solve the problem.

7. The museum has 81 pictures displayed. There are 9 pictures hanging in each room. How many rooms are there?

   _____

8. Brian has 10 friends at his party. He gives each friend 5 baseball cards. How many baseball cards does he give his friends?

   _____

9. **Stretch Your Thinking** Anita wants to buy a box of glitter packets to divide evenly among her three art classes. She doesn't want any glitter packets left over. Which box of glitter packets should Anita buy?

35 packets   27 packets   19 packets

   _____

   _____

   _____

Multiply and Divide with 3

2×2

$$\begin{array}{r} 2 \\ \times\, 3 \end{array} \qquad \begin{array}{r} 3 \\ \times\, 2 \end{array}$$

2×4
4×2

$$\begin{array}{r} 2 \\ \times\, 5 \end{array} \qquad \begin{array}{r} 5 \\ \times\, 2 \end{array}$$

2×6
6×2

$$\begin{array}{r} 2 \\ \times\, 7 \end{array} \qquad \begin{array}{r} 7 \\ \times\, 2 \end{array}$$

2×8
8×2

$$\begin{array}{r} 2 \\ \times\, 9 \end{array} \qquad \begin{array}{r} 9 \\ \times\, 2 \end{array}$$

$10 = 2 \times 5$

$10 = 5 \times 2$

5	2
10	4
	6
	8
	10

5
2 [10]

$\begin{array}{r} 2 \\ \times 4 \\ \hline 8 \end{array}$

$\begin{array}{r} 4 \\ \times 2 \\ \hline 8 \end{array}$

2	4
4	8
6	
8	

2
4 [8]

$6 = 2 \times 3$

$6 = 3 \times 2$

3	2
6	4
	6

3
2 [6]

$\begin{array}{r} 2 \\ \times 2 \\ \hline 4 \end{array}$

2
4

2
2 [4]

$18 = 2 \times 9$

$18 = 9 \times 2$

9	2
18	4
	6
	8
	10
	12
	14
	16
	18

9
2 [18]

$\begin{array}{r} 2 \\ \times 8 \\ \hline 16 \end{array}$

$\begin{array}{r} 8 \\ \times 2 \\ \hline 16 \end{array}$

8	2
16	4
	6
	8
	10
	12
	14
	16

2
8 [16]

$14 = 2 \times 7$

$14 = 7 \times 2$

7	2
14	4
	6
	8
	10
	12
	14

7
2 [14]

$\begin{array}{r} 2 \\ \times 6 \\ \hline 12 \end{array}$

$\begin{array}{r} 6 \\ \times 2 \\ \hline 12 \end{array}$

6	2
12	4
	6
	8
	10
	12

2
6 [12]

Home Multiplication Strategy Cards

3×3

$$\begin{array}{r} 3 \\ \times\ 4 \\ \hline \end{array} \qquad \begin{array}{r} 4 \\ \times\ 3 \\ \hline \end{array}$$

3×5
5×3

$$\begin{array}{r} 3 \\ \times\ 6 \\ \hline \end{array} \qquad \begin{array}{r} 6 \\ \times\ 3 \\ \hline \end{array}$$

3×7
7×3

$$\begin{array}{r} 3 \\ \times\ 8 \\ \hline \end{array} \qquad \begin{array}{r} 8 \\ \times\ 3 \\ \hline \end{array}$$

3×9
9×3

$$\begin{array}{r} 4 \\ \times\ 4 \\ \hline \end{array}$$

$18 = 3 \times 6$

$18 = 6 \times 3$

6	3
12	6
18	9
	12
	15
	18

6

3 • 18

$\begin{array}{r} 3 \\ \times 5 \\ \hline 15 \end{array}$ $\begin{array}{r} 5 \\ \times 3 \\ \hline 15 \end{array}$

5	3
10	6
15	9
	12
	15

3

5 • 15

$12 = 3 \times 4$

$12 = 4 \times 3$

4	3
8	6
12	9
	12

4

3 • 12

$\begin{array}{r} 3 \\ \times 3 \\ \hline 9 \end{array}$

3
6
9

3

3 • 9

$16 = 4 \times 4$

4
8
12
16

4

4 • 16

$\begin{array}{r} 3 \\ \times 9 \\ \hline 27 \end{array}$ $\begin{array}{r} 9 \\ \times 3 \\ \hline 27 \end{array}$

9	3
18	6
27	9
	12
	15
	18
	21
	24
	27

9

3 • 27

$24 = 3 \times 8$

$24 = 8 \times 3$

8	3
16	6
24	9
	12
	15
	18
	21
	24

3

8 • 24

$\begin{array}{r} 3 \\ \times 7 \\ \hline 21 \end{array}$ $\begin{array}{r} 7 \\ \times 3 \\ \hline 21 \end{array}$

7	3
14	6
21	9
	12
	15
	18
	21

7

3 • 21

Home Multiplication Strategy Cards

4×5
5×4

$\begin{array}{r} 4 \\ \times\ 6 \end{array}$ $\begin{array}{r} 6 \\ \times\ 4 \end{array}$

4×7
7×4

$\begin{array}{r} 4 \\ \times\ 8 \end{array}$ $\begin{array}{r} 8 \\ \times\ 4 \end{array}$

4×9
9×4

$\begin{array}{r} 5 \\ \times\ 5 \end{array}$

5×6
6×5

$\begin{array}{r} 5 \\ \times\ 7 \end{array}$ $\begin{array}{r} 7 \\ \times\ 5 \end{array}$

$32 = 4 \times 8$

$32 = 8 \times 4$

8	4
16	8
24	12
32	16
	20
	24
	28
	32

4

8 | 32

$\begin{array}{r} 4 \\ \times 7 \\ \hline 28 \end{array}$ $\begin{array}{r} 7 \\ \times 4 \\ \hline 28 \end{array}$

7	4
14	8
21	12
28	16
	20
	24
	28

7

4 | 28

$24 = 4 \times 6$

$24 = 6 \times 4$

6	4
12	8
18	12
24	16
	20
	24

4

6 | 24

$\begin{array}{r} 4 \\ \times 5 \\ \hline 20 \end{array}$ $\begin{array}{r} 5 \\ \times 4 \\ \hline 20 \end{array}$

5	4
10	8
15	12
20	16
	20

5

4 | 20

$35 = 5 \times 7$

$35 = 7 \times 5$

7	5
14	10
21	15
28	20
35	25
	30
	35

7

5 | 35

$\begin{array}{r} 5 \\ \times 6 \\ \hline 30 \end{array}$ $\begin{array}{r} 6 \\ \times 5 \\ \hline 30 \end{array}$

6	5
12	10
18	15
24	20
30	25
	30

5

6 | 30

$25 = 5 \times 5$

5
10
15
20
25

5

5 | 25

$\begin{array}{r} 4 \\ \times 9 \\ \hline 36 \end{array}$ $\begin{array}{r} 9 \\ \times 4 \\ \hline 36 \end{array}$

9	4
18	8
27	12
36	16
	20
	24
	28
	32
	36

9

4 | 36

Home Multiplication Strategy Cards

5×8
8×5

$\begin{array}{r} 5 \\ \times 9 \\ \hline \end{array}$ $\begin{array}{r} 9 \\ \times 5 \\ \hline \end{array}$

6×6

$\begin{array}{r} 6 \\ \times 7 \\ \hline \end{array}$ $\begin{array}{r} 7 \\ \times 6 \\ \hline \end{array}$

6×8
8×6

$\begin{array}{r} 6 \\ \times 9 \\ \hline \end{array}$ $\begin{array}{r} 9 \\ \times 6 \\ \hline \end{array}$

7×7

$\begin{array}{r} 7 \\ \times 8 \\ \hline \end{array}$ $\begin{array}{r} 8 \\ \times 7 \\ \hline \end{array}$

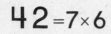

42 = 7 × 6
42 = 6 × 7

6	7
12	14
18	21
24	28
30	35
36	42
42	

7
6 | 42

6
× 6
___
36

6
12
18
24
30
36
6

6 | 36

45 = 9 × 5
45 = 5 × 9

5	9
10	18
15	27
20	36
25	45
30	
35	
40	
45	

9
5 | 45

8
× 5
___
40

5
× 8
___
40

5
10
15
20
25
30
35
40

5
8 | 40

56 = 7 × 8
56 = 8 × 7

8	7
16	14
24	21
32	28
40	35
48	42
56	49
	56

8
7 | 56

7
× 7
___
49

7
14
21
28
35
42
49
7

7 | 49

54 = 9 × 6
54 = 6 × 9

6	9
12	18
18	27
24	36
30	45
36	54
42	
48	
54	

9
6 | 54

6
× 8
___
48

8
× 6
___
48

6	8
12	16
18	24
24	32
30	40
36	48
42	
48	

8
6 | 48

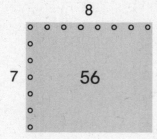
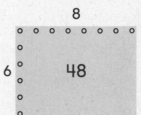

Home Multiplication Strategy Cards

7×9
9×7

$$\begin{array}{r} 8 \\ \times\ 8 \\ \hline \end{array}$$

9×8
8×9

$$\begin{array}{r} 9 \\ \times\ 9 \\ \hline \end{array}$$

Card 1

$81 = 9 \times 9$

9
18
27
36
45

54
63
72
81

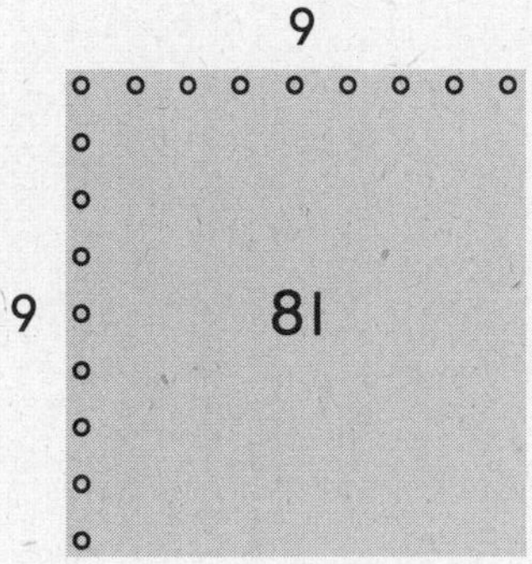

9 × 9 = 81

Card 2

$$9 \times 8 = 72 \qquad 8 \times 9 = 72$$

8   9
16   18
24   27
32   36
40   45

48   54
56   63
64   72
72

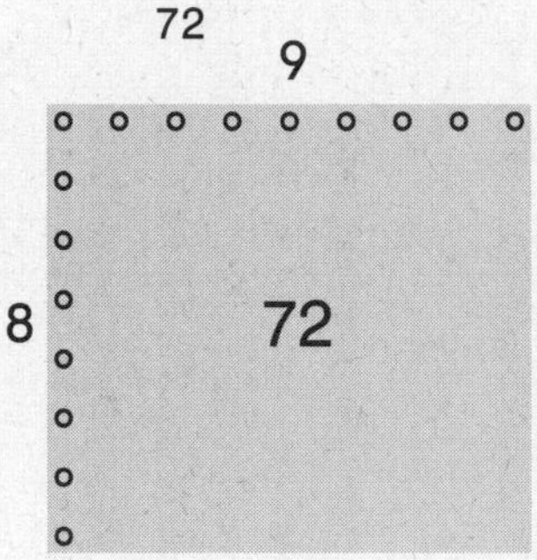

8 × 9 = 72

Card 3

$64 = 8 \times 8$

8
16
24
32
40

48
56
64

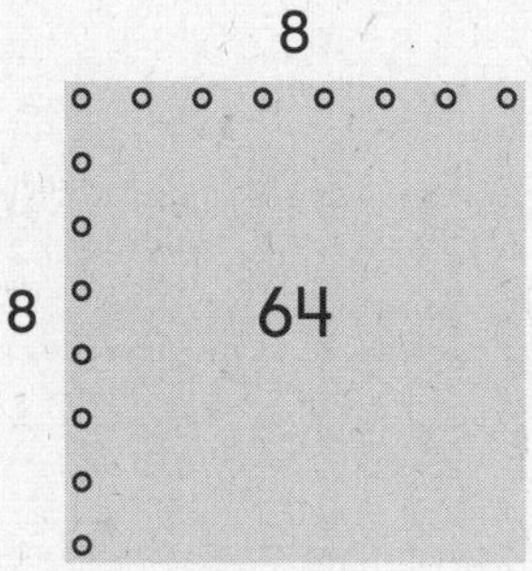

8 × 8 = 64

Card 4

$$7 \times 9 = 63 \qquad 9 \times 7 = 63$$

9   7
18   14
27   21
36   28
45   35

54   42
63   49
      56
      63

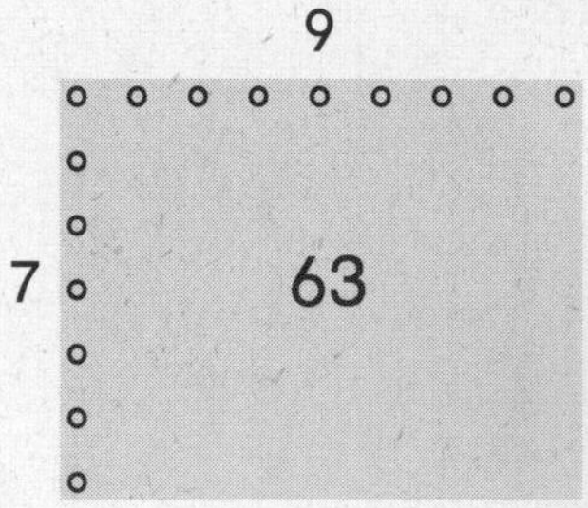

7 × 9 = 63

Home Multiplication Strategy Cards

$2\overline{)4}$

$4 \div 2$

$2\overline{)6}$

$6 \div 2$

$2\overline{)8}$

$8 \div 2$

$2\overline{)10}$

$10 \div 2$

$2\overline{)12}$

$12 \div 2$

$2\overline{)14}$

$14 \div 2$

$2\overline{)16}$

$16 \div 2$

$2\overline{)18}$

$18 \div 2$

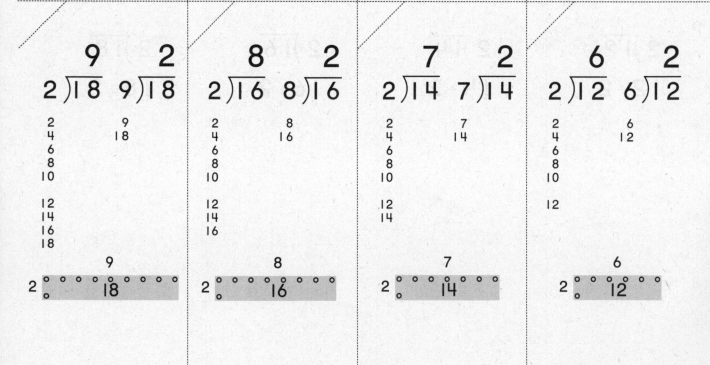

5 2)10   2 5)10
2
4
6
8
10
       5
       10

5
2) 10

4 2)8   2 4)8
2
4
6
8
       4
       8

4
2) 8

3 2)6   2 3)6
2
4
6
       3
       6

3
2) 6

2 2)4
2
4

2
2) 4

9 2)18   2 9)18
2
4
6
8
10

12
14
16
18
       9
       18

9
2) 18

8 2)16   2 8)16
2
4
6
8
10

12
14
16
       8
       16

8
2) 16

7 2)14   2 7)14
2
4
6
8
10

12
14
       7
       14

7
2) 14

6 2)12   2 6)12
2
4
6
8
10

12
       6
       12

6
2) 12

Home Division Strategy Cards

$3\overline{)6}$

$6 \div 3$

$4\overline{)8}$

$8 \div 4$

$5\overline{)10}$

$10 \div 5$

$6\overline{)12}$

$12 \div 6$

$7\overline{)14}$

$14 \div 7$

$8\overline{)16}$

$16 \div 8$

$9\overline{)18}$

$18 \div 9$

$3\overline{)9}$

$9 \div 3$

2 | **6**
6)12 | 2)12

6
12

2
4
6
8
10

12

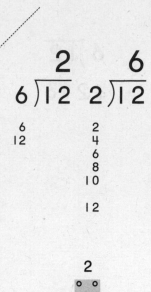

2
6 12

---

2 | **5**
5)10 | 2)10

5
10

2
4
6
8
10

2
5 10

---

2 | **4**
4)8 | 2)8

4
8

2
4
6
8

2
4 8

---

2 | **3**
3)6 | 2)6

3
6

2
4
6

2
3 6

3
3)9

3
6
9

3
3 9

---

2 | **9**
9)18 | 2)18

9
18

2
4
6
8
10

12
14
16
18

2
9 18

---

2 | **8**
8)16 | 2)16

8
16

2
4
6
8
10

12
14
16

2
8 16

---

2 | **7**
7)14 | 2)14

7
14

2
4
6
8
10

12
14

2
7 14

$3\overline{)12}$

$12 \div 3$

$3\overline{)15}$

$15 \div 3$

$3\overline{)18}$

$18 \div 3$

$3\overline{)21}$

$21 \div 3$

$3\overline{)24}$

$24 \div 3$

$3\overline{)27}$

$27 \div 3$

$4\overline{)12}$

$12 \div 4$

$5\overline{)15}$

$15 \div 5$

7 **3**

3)21 7)21

3   7
6   14
9   21
12
15

18
21

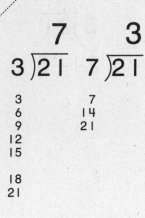

7
3 · 21

6 **3**

3)18 6)18

3   6
6   12
9   18
12
15

18

6
3 · 18

5 **3**

3)15 5)15

3   5
6   10
9   15
12
15

5
3 · 15

4 **3**

3)12 4)12

3   4
6   8
9   12
12

4
3 · 12

---

3 **5**

5)15 3)15

5   3
10   6
15   9
     12
     15

3
5 · 15

3 **4**

4)12 3)12

4   3
8   6
12   9
     12

3
4 · 12

9 **3**

3)27 9)27

3   9
6   18
9   27
12
15

18
21
24
27

9
3 · 27

8 **3**

3)24 8)24

3   8
6   16
9   24
12
15

18
21
24

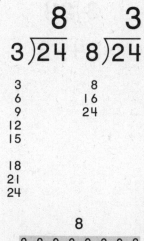
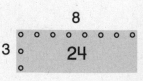

8
3 · 24

Home Division Strategy Cards

$6\overline{)18}$ $7\overline{)21}$ $8\overline{)24}$ $9\overline{)27}$

$18 \div 6$ $21 \div 7$ $24 \div 8$ $27 \div 9$

$4\overline{)16}$ $4\overline{)20}$ $4\overline{)24}$ $4\overline{)28}$

$16 \div 4$ $20 \div 4$ $24 \div 4$ $28 \div 4$

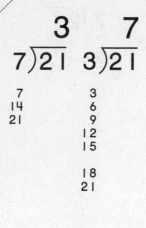

$$3 \quad\quad 9$$
$$9\overline{)27} \quad 3\overline{)27}$$

9	3
18	6
27	9
	12
	15
	18
	21
	24
	27

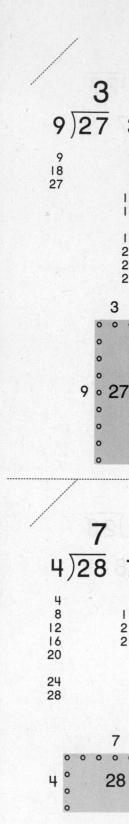

3

9 ° 27

$$3 \quad\quad 8$$
$$8\overline{)24} \quad 3\overline{)24}$$

8	3
16	6
24	9
	12
	15
	18
	21
	24

3

8 ° 24

$$3 \quad\quad 7$$
$$7\overline{)21} \quad 3\overline{)21}$$

7	3
14	6
21	9
	12
	15
	18
	21

3

7 ° 21

$$3 \quad\quad 6$$
$$6\overline{)18} \quad 3\overline{)18}$$

6	3
12	6
18	9
	12
	15
	18

3

6 ° 18

$$7 \quad\quad 4$$
$$4\overline{)28} \quad 7\overline{)28}$$

4	7
8	14
12	21
16	28
20	
24	
28	

7

4 ° 28

$$6 \quad\quad 4$$
$$4\overline{)24} \quad 6\overline{)24}$$

4	6
8	12
12	18
16	24
20	
24	

6

4 ° 24

$$5 \quad\quad 4$$
$$4\overline{)20} \quad 5\overline{)20}$$

4	5
8	10
12	15
16	20
20	

5

4 ° 20

$$4$$
$$4\overline{)16}$$

4
8
12
16

4

4 ° 16

Home Division Strategy Cards

$4\overline{)32}$
$32 \div 4$

$4\overline{)36}$
$36 \div 4$

$5\overline{)20}$
$20 \div 5$

$6\overline{)24}$
$24 \div 6$

$7\overline{)28}$
$28 \div 7$

$8\overline{)32}$
$32 \div 8$

$9\overline{)36}$
$36 \div 9$

$5\overline{)25}$
$25 \div 5$

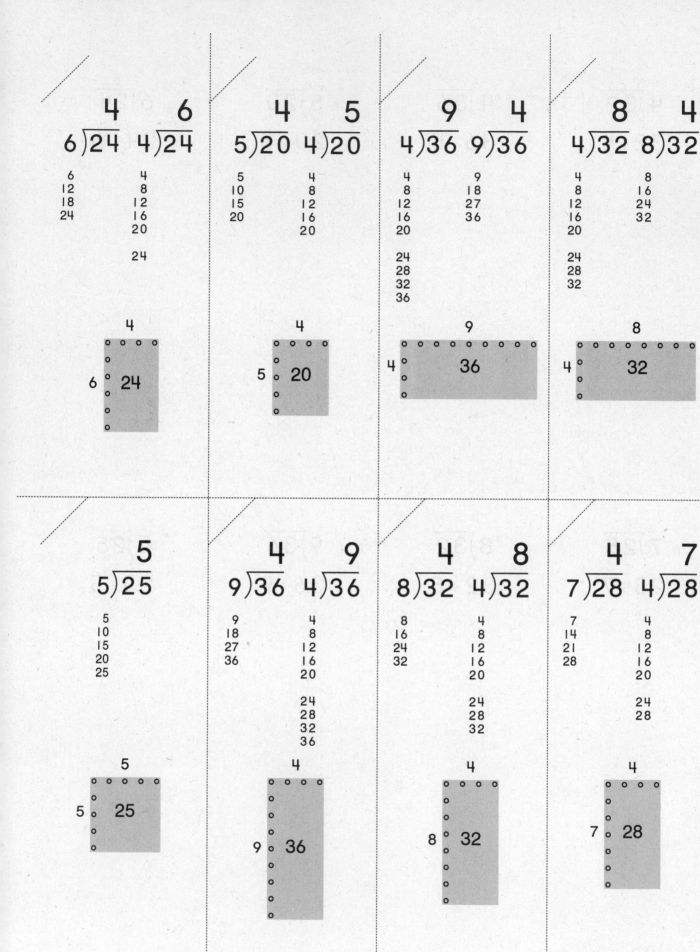

Home Division Strategy Cards

$5\overline{)30}$

$30 \div 5$

$5\overline{)35}$

$35 \div 5$

$5\overline{)40}$

$40 \div 5$

$5\overline{)45}$

$45 \div 5$

$6\overline{)30}$

$30 \div 6$

$7\overline{)35}$

$35 \div 7$

$8\overline{)40}$

$40 \div 8$

$9\overline{)45}$

$45 \div 9$

9 **5**

5)45 9)45

5	9
10	18
15	27
20	36
25	45
30	
35	
40	
45	

9

5 | 45

8 **5**

5)40 8)40

5	8
10	16
15	24
20	32
25	40
30	
35	
40	

8

5 | 40

7 **5**

5)35 7)35

5	7
10	14
15	21
20	28
25	35
30	
35	

7

5 | 35

6 **5**

5)30 6)30

5	6
10	12
15	18
20	24
25	30
30	

6

5 | 30

5 **9**

9)45 5)45

9	5
18	10
27	15
36	20
45	25
	30
	35
	40
	45

5

9 | 45

5 **8**

8)40 5)40

8	5
16	10
24	15
32	20
40	25
	30
	35
	40

5

8 | 40

5 **7**

7)35 5)35

7	5
14	10
21	15
28	20
35	25
	30
	35

5

7 | 35

5 **6**

6)30 5)30

6	5
12	10
18	15
24	20
30	25
	30

5

6 | 30

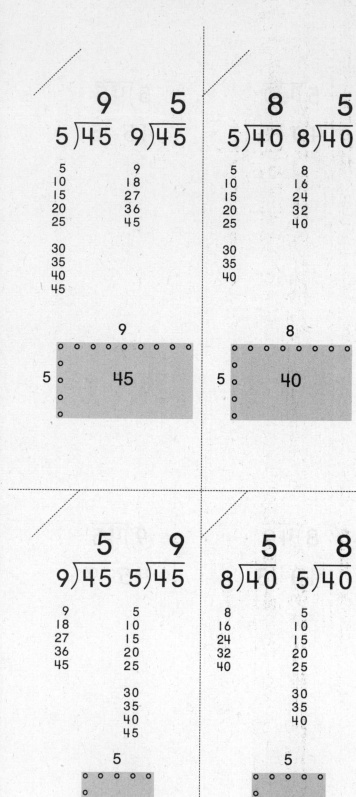
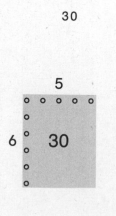

© Houghton Mifflin Harcourt Publishing Company

Home Division Strategy Cards

$6\overline{)36}$

$36 \div 6$

$6\overline{)42}$

$42 \div 6$

$6\overline{)48}$

$48 \div 6$

$6\overline{)54}$

$54 \div 6$

$7\overline{)42}$

$42 \div 7$

$8\overline{)48}$

$48 \div 8$

$9\overline{)54}$

$54 \div 9$

$7\overline{)49}$

$49 \div 7$

Card 1

9 6
$6)\overline{54}$ $9)\overline{54}$

6	9
12	18
18	27
24	36
30	45
36	54
42	
48	
54	

9

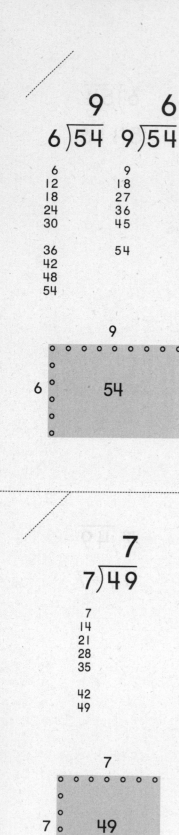

6 54

Card 2

8 6
$6)\overline{48}$ $8)\overline{48}$

6	8
12	16
18	24
24	32
30	40
36	48
42	
48	

8

6 48

Card 3

7 6
$6)\overline{42}$ $7)\overline{42}$

6	7
12	14
18	21
24	28
30	35
36	42
42	

7

6 42

Card 4

6
$6)\overline{36}$

6
12
18
24
30
36

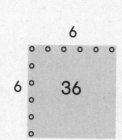

6

6 36

Card 5

7
$7)\overline{49}$

7
14
21
28
35
42
49

7

7 49

Card 6

6 9
$9)\overline{54}$ $6)\overline{54}$

9	6
18	12
27	18
36	24
45	30
54	36
	42
	48
	54

6

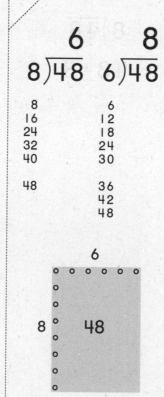

9 54

Card 7

6 8
$8)\overline{48}$ $6)\overline{48}$

8	6
16	12
24	18
32	24
40	30
48	36
	42
	48

6

8 48

Card 8

6 7
$7)\overline{42}$ $6)\overline{42}$

7	6
14	12
21	18
28	24
35	30
42	36
	42

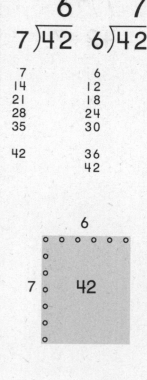

6

7 42

Home Division Strategy Cards

$7\overline{)56}$

$56 \div 7$

$7\overline{)63}$

$63 \div 7$

$8\overline{)56}$

$56 \div 8$

$9\overline{)63}$

$63 \div 9$

$8\overline{)64}$

$64 \div 8$

$8\overline{)72}$

$72 \div 8$

$9\overline{)72}$

$72 \div 9$

$9\overline{)81}$

$81 \div 9$

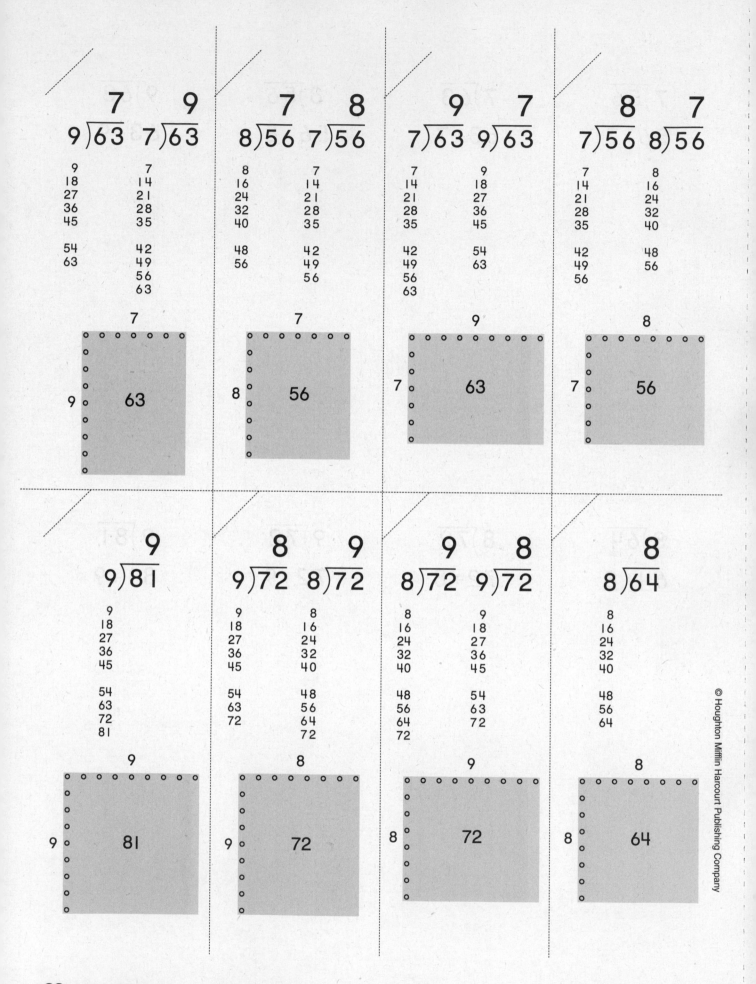

Homework

Name _____ Date _____

© Houghton Mifflin Harcourt Publishing Company

Home Study Sheet B

4s

Count-bys	Mixed Up ×	Mixed Up ÷
1 × 4 = 4	4 × 4 = 16	12 ÷ 4 = 3
2 × 4 = 8	1 × 4 = 4	36 ÷ 4 = 9
3 × 4 = 12	7 × 4 = 28	24 ÷ 4 = 6
4 × 4 = 16	3 × 4 = 12	4 ÷ 4 = 1
5 × 4 = 20	9 × 4 = 36	20 ÷ 4 = 5
6 × 4 = 24	10 × 4 = 40	28 ÷ 4 = 7
7 × 4 = 28	2 × 4 = 8	8 ÷ 4 = 2
8 × 4 = 32	5 × 4 = 20	40 ÷ 4 = 10
9 × 4 = 36	8 × 4 = 32	32 ÷ 4 = 8
10 × 4 = 40	6 × 4 = 24	16 ÷ 4 = 4

1s

Count-bys	Mixed Up ×	Mixed Up ÷
1 × 1 = 1	5 × 1 = 5	10 ÷ 1 = 10
2 × 1 = 2	7 × 1 = 7	8 ÷ 1 = 8
3 × 1 = 3	10 × 1 = 10	4 ÷ 1 = 4
4 × 1 = 4	1 × 1 = 1	9 ÷ 1 = 9
5 × 1 = 5	8 × 1 = 8	6 ÷ 1 = 6
6 × 1 = 6	4 × 1 = 4	7 ÷ 1 = 7
7 × 1 = 7	9 × 1 = 9	1 ÷ 1 = 1
8 × 1 = 8	3 × 1 = 3	2 ÷ 1 = 2
9 × 1 = 9	2 × 1 = 2	5 ÷ 1 = 5
10 × 1 = 10	6 × 1 = 6	3 ÷ 1 = 3

3s

Count-bys	Mixed Up ×	Mixed Up ÷
1 × 3 = 3	5 × 3 = 15	27 ÷ 3 = 9
2 × 3 = 6	1 × 3 = 3	6 ÷ 3 = 2
3 × 3 = 9	8 × 3 = 24	18 ÷ 3 = 6
4 × 3 = 12	10 × 3 = 30	30 ÷ 3 = 10
5 × 3 = 15	3 × 3 = 9	9 ÷ 3 = 3
6 × 3 = 18	7 × 3 = 21	3 ÷ 3 = 1
7 × 3 = 21	9 × 3 = 27	12 ÷ 3 = 4
8 × 3 = 24	2 × 3 = 6	24 ÷ 3 = 8
9 × 3 = 27	4 × 3 = 12	15 ÷ 3 = 5
10 × 3 = 30	6 × 3 = 18	21 ÷ 3 = 7

0s

Count-bys	Mixed Up ×
1 × 0 = 0	3 × 0 = 0
2 × 0 = 0	10 × 0 = 0
3 × 0 = 0	5 × 0 = 0
4 × 0 = 0	8 × 0 = 0
5 × 0 = 0	7 × 0 = 0
6 × 0 = 0	2 × 0 = 0
7 × 0 = 0	9 × 0 = 0
8 × 0 = 0	6 × 0 = 0
9 × 0 = 0	1 × 0 = 0
10 × 0 = 0	4 × 0 = 0

Homework

Multiply or divide to find the unknown numbers. Then check your answers at the bottom of the page.

1. $3 \times 5 = \boxed{}$

2. $27 \div 9 = \boxed{}$

3. $2\overline{)20}$ with $\boxed{}$ above

4. $7 \cdot 9 = \boxed{}$

5. $2 * \boxed{} = 12$

6. $18 / 3 = \boxed{}$

7. $9 \times 5 = \boxed{}$

8. $3 * \boxed{} = 21$

9. $\frac{81}{9} = \boxed{}$

10. $6 \div 3 = \boxed{}$

11. $8 \times 2 = \boxed{}$

12. $\frac{14}{2} = \boxed{}$

13. $3 \cdot 3 = \boxed{}$

14. $\boxed{} * 9 = 72$

15. $90 \div 9 = \boxed{}$

16. $\boxed{} * 2 = 18$

17. $24 \div \boxed{} = 8$

18. $12 / \boxed{} = 6$

19. $6 \cdot 5 = \boxed{}$

20. $4 \times \boxed{} = 40$

21. $\boxed{} \cdot 9 = 54$

1. 15 2. 3 3. 10 4. 63 5. 6 6. 6 7. 45 8. 7 9. 9 10. 2 11. 16
12. 7 13. 9 14. 8 15. 10 16. 9 17. 3 18. 2 19. 30 20. 10 21. 6

Name _____ **Date** _____

Homework

Study Plan
Homework Helper

Make a rectangle drawing to represent each exercise.
Then find the product.

1. $5 \times 9 =$ _____   **2.** $3 * 6 =$ _____   **3.** $3 \cdot 9 =$ _____

Ashley drew this large rectangle, which is made up of two small rectangles.

4. Find the area of the large rectangle by finding the areas of the two small rectangles and adding them.

_____

_____

5. Find the area of the large rectangle by multiplying the number of rows by the number of square units in each row.

_____

6. Find this product: $5 \times 6 =$ _____

7. Find this product: $2 \times 6 =$ _____

8. Use your answers to exercises 6 and 7 to find this product: $7 \times 6 =$ _____

Name _____ **Date** _____

Remembering

Multiply or divide to find the unknown numbers.

1. $30 \div 3 =$ ☐

2. $5 * $ ☐ $= 40$

3. $\frac{18}{9} =$ ☐

4. $3 \cdot 8 =$ ☐

5. $5\overline{)25}$ ☐

6. ☐ $\times 2 = 14$

Write an equation and solve the problem.

7. There are 50 paper clips in the box. Each art project requires 10 paper clips. How many art projects can be made with the box of 50 clips?

_____

8. There are 27 toys in 3 boxes. Each box has the same number of toys. How many toys are in each box?

_____

Find the total number by starting with the third count-by and counting from there.

9. How many triangles are in these 7 sets?

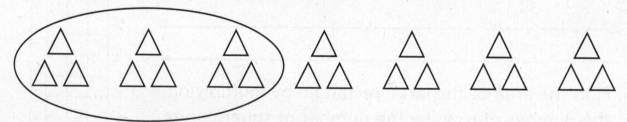

_____   _____   _____

10. **Stretch Your Thinking** Aiden knows the length of only one side of his garden. He says he will be able to find the area knowing only one side. Explain how this can be true.

_____

_____

_____

Multiplication and Area

Homework

Use this table to practice your 4s count-bys, multiplications, and divisions. Then have your Homework Helper test you.

	× In Order	× Mixed Up	÷ Mixed Up
4s	$1 \times 4 = 4$	$9 \times 4 = 36$	$20 \div 4 = 5$
	$2 \times 4 = 8$	$5 \times 4 = 20$	$4 \div 4 = 1$
	$3 \times 4 = 12$	$7 \times 4 = 28$	$16 \div 4 = 4$
	$4 \times 4 = 16$	$2 \times 4 = 8$	$36 \div 4 = 9$
	$5 \times 4 = 20$	$4 \times 4 = 16$	$24 \div 4 = 6$
	$6 \times 4 = 24$	$1 \times 4 = 4$	$12 \div 4 = 3$
	$7 \times 4 = 28$	$6 \times 4 = 24$	$32 \div 4 = 8$
	$8 \times 4 = 32$	$8 \times 4 = 32$	$8 \div 4 = 2$
	$9 \times 4 = 36$	$3 \times 4 = 12$	$40 \div 4 = 10$
	$10 \times 4 = 40$	$10 \times 4 = 40$	$28 \div 4 = 7$

Multiply and Divide with 4

Homework

Multiply or divide to find the unknown numbers. Then check your answers at the bottom of this page.

1. $4 \times 9 =$ ☐

2. $12 \div 3 =$ ☐

3. $4 * 8 =$ ☐

4. $30 / 3 =$ ☐

5. $3 \bullet$ ☐ $= 24$

6. $9\overline{)81}$ ☐

7. $6 \times 3 =$ ☐

8. $\frac{27}{3} =$ ☐

9. $9 \times 10 =$ ☐

10. $24 / 4 =$ ☐

11. $10 \bullet 3 =$ ☐

12. $16 \div 4 =$ ☐

13. $9 *$ ☐ $= 63$

14. $\frac{36}{4} =$ ☐

15. $7 \bullet 4 =$ ☐

16. $20 / 4 =$ ☐

17. $9\overline{)54}$ ☐

18. $3 * 7 =$ ☐

19. ☐ $\times 4 = 4$

20. $15 \div 3 =$ ☐

21. $4 \times$ ☐ $= 16$

1. 36 2. 4 3. 32 4. 10 5. 8 6. 9 7. 18 8. 9 9. 90 10. 6 11. 30
12. 4 13. 7 14. 9 15. 28 16. 5 17. 6 18. 21 19. 1 20. 5 21. 4

Multiply and Divide with 4

Homework

Home Check Sheet 4: 3s and 4s

3s Multiplication	3s Divisions	4s Multiplications	4s Divisions
$8 \times 3 = 24$	$9 / 3 = 3$	$1 \times 4 = 4$	$40 / 4 = 10$
$3 \cdot 2 = 6$	$21 \div 3 = 7$	$4 \cdot 5 = 20$	$12 \div 4 = 3$
$3 * 5 = 15$	$27 / 3 = 9$	$8 * 4 = 32$	$24 / 4 = 6$
$10 \times 3 = 30$	$3 \div 3 = 1$	$3 \times 4 = 12$	$8 \div 4 = 2$
$3 \cdot 3 = 9$	$18 / 3 = 6$	$4 \cdot 6 = 24$	$4 / 4 = 1$
$3 * 6 = 18$	$12 \div 3 = 4$	$4 * 9 = 36$	$28 \div 4 = 7$
$7 \times 3 = 21$	$30 / 3 = 10$	$10 \times 4 = 40$	$32 / 4 = 8$
$3 \cdot 9 = 27$	$6 \div 3 = 2$	$4 \cdot 7 = 28$	$16 \div 4 = 4$
$4 * 3 = 12$	$24 / 3 = 8$	$4 * 4 = 16$	$36 / 4 = 9$
$3 \times 1 = 3$	$15 / 3 = 5$	$2 \times 4 = 8$	$20 / 4 = 5$
$3 \cdot 4 = 12$	$21 \div 3 = 7$	$4 \cdot 3 = 12$	$4 \div 4 = 1$
$3 * 3 = 9$	$3 / 3 = 1$	$4 * 2 = 8$	$32 / 4 = 8$
$3 \times 10 = 30$	$9 \div 3 = 3$	$9 \times 4 = 36$	$8 \div 4 = 2$
$2 \cdot 3 = 6$	$27 / 3 = 9$	$1 \cdot 4 = 4$	$16 / 4 = 4$
$3 * 7 = 21$	$30 \div 3 = 10$	$4 * 6 = 24$	$36 \div 4 = 9$
$6 \times 3 = 18$	$18 / 3 = 6$	$5 \times 4 = 20$	$12 / 4 = 3$
$5 \cdot 3 = 15$	$6 \div 3 = 2$	$4 \cdot 4 = 16$	$40 \div 4 = 10$
$3 * 8 = 24$	$15 \div 3 = 5$	$7 * 4 = 28$	$20 \div 4 = 5$
$9 \times 3 = 27$	$12 / 3 = 4$	$8 \times 4 = 32$	$24 / 4 = 6$
$2 \cdot 3 = 6$	$24 \div 3 = 8$	$10 \cdot 4 = 40$	$28 \div 4 = 7$

Name _____ **Date** _____

Homework

© Houghton Mifflin Harcourt Publishing Company

Study Plan

Homework Helper _____

Solve each problem.

1. Colin had 16 puzzles. He gave 4 puzzles to each of his nephews. How many nephews does Colin have?

_____

2. Allegra listed the names of her classmates in 4 columns, with 7 names in each column. How many classmates does Allegra have?

_____

This large rectangle is made up of two small rectangles.

3. Find the area of the large rectangle by finding the areas of the two small rectangles and adding them.

_____

4. Find the area of the large rectangle by multiplying the number of rows by the number of square units in each row.

_____

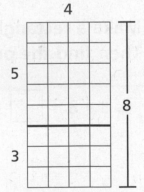

This Equal-Shares drawing shows that 6 groups of 9 is the same as 5 groups of 9 plus 1 group of 9.

5. Find $5 \times ⑨$ and $1 \times ⑨$, and add the answers.

_____

6. Find $6 \times ⑨$. Did you get the same answer as in question 5?

_____

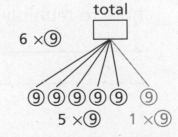

Remembering

Multiply or divide to find the unknown numbers.

1. $18 \div 2 = \boxed{}$

2. $9 * \boxed{} = 72$

3. $\dfrac{40}{5} = \boxed{}$

4. $2 \cdot 7 = \boxed{}$

5. $5\overline{)30}^{\,\boxed{}}$

6. $\boxed{} \times 10 = 70$

Write an equation and solve the problem.

7. Sydney has piles of 10 sticker sheets. She has 100 sheets in all. How many piles does she have?

_____

8. Mr. Thomas gives 4 crayons to each of 8 students. How many crayons does he give out?

_____

Make a rectangle drawing to represent each multiplication. Then find the product.

9. $3 \cdot 8 = \boxed{}$

10. $2 \cdot 9 = \boxed{}$

11. **Stretch Your Thinking** Explain how you can solve 8×8 if you know how to multiply with 4 but not how to multiply with 8.

_____

_____

Homework

Study Plan

_____

Homework Helper

Write an equation and solve the problem.

1. Pablo hung his watercolor paintings in an array with 3 rows and 4 columns. How many paintings did Pablo hang?

_____

2. A group of 7 friends went on a hiking trip. Each person took 3 granola bars. What total number of granola bars did the friends take?

_____

3. Jon had 45 sheets of construction paper. He used 9 sheets to make paper snowflakes. How many sheets does he have now?

_____

You can combine multiplications you know to find multiplications you don't know.

4. Find this product: $5 \times 8 =$ _____

5. Find this product: $1 \times 8 =$ _____

6. Use the answers to Exercises 4 and 5 to find this product: $6 \times 8 =$ _____

Name   Date

Remembering

Write an equation and solve the problem.

1. Tamara has 3 soccer practices each week. How many practices will she have after 7 weeks?

   _____

2. David has 24 items to put in bags. If he puts 3 items in each bag, how many bags does he need?

   _____

Solve each problem.

The Equal Shares drawing at the right shows that 8 groups of 4 is the same as 7 groups of 4 plus 1 group of 4.

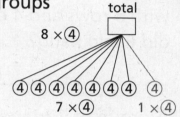

3. Find $7 \times \textcircled{4}$ and $1 \times \textcircled{4}$. Then add the answers.

   _____

4. Find $8 \times \textcircled{4}$. Did you get the same answer as in exercise 3?

   _____

5. Find the area of the large rectangle by finding the area of the two small rectangles and adding them.

   _____

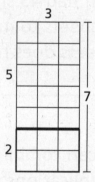

6. Find the area of the large rectangle by multiplying the number of rows by the number of squares in each row.

   _____

7. **Stretch Your Thinking** Select a strategy card. Without looking at the back, write two strategies you can use to solve it. Turn it over to check.

   _____

   _____

Use the Strategy Cards

Homework

Study Plan

_____

Homework Helper

Multiply or divide to find the unknown numbers.

1. 4 * 3 = _____

2. 4 × _____ = 28

3. 27 ÷ 9 = _____

4. 30 / 5 = _____

5. 9 • 9 = _____

6. 8 × _____ = 16

7. 3 • _____ = 18

8. 21 ÷ 3 = _____

9. 45 / 5 = _____

Write an equation and solve the problem.   *Show your work.*

10. There are 4 measuring cups in a set. Mr. Lee's science class has 8 sets of measuring cups. How many cups are there altogether?

_____

11. A carousel has 40 horses. There are 4 horses in each row. How many rows are there on the carousel?

_____

12. Kevin said it is 2 weeks until his birthday. A week is 7 days. How many days is it until Kevin's birthday?

_____

Name _____ Date _____

Remembering

1. Find this product: $3 \times 9 =$ _____

2. Find this product: $5 \times 9 =$ _____

3. Use your answers to Exercises 1 and 2 to find this product: $8 \times 9 =$ _____

Multiply or divide to find the unknown numbers.

4. $3 \cdot 6 = \boxed{}$

5. $5\overline{)40}$ with $\boxed{}$ above

6. $\boxed{} \times 4 = 28$

7. $32 \div 8 = \boxed{}$

8. $5 * \boxed{} = 35$

9. $\dfrac{16}{4} = \boxed{}$

10. $\dfrac{16}{2} = \boxed{}$

11. $30 \div \boxed{} = 3$

12. $4 \times \boxed{} = 12$

Write an equation and solve the problem.

13. Lauren uses 30 beads to make 5 bracelets. She uses the same number of beads for each bracelet. How many beads are on each bracelet?

_____

14. Eric sets up chairs for a meeting in 6 rows of 9. How many chairs does he set up?

_____

15. Stretch Your Thinking Suppose your teacher tells you to write a word problem using the number 3. Which would be the best object to use in your problem? Explain. Then write and solve a word problem using that object.

    tricycle   **bike**   **wagon**

_____

_____

         Building Fluency with 2s, 3s, 4s, 5s, 9s, and 10s

Homework

1s

× In Order	× Mixed Up	÷ Mixed Up
$1 \times 1 = 1$	$3 \times 1 = 3$	$7 \div 1 = 7$
$2 \times 1 = 2$	$7 \times 1 = 7$	$10 \div 1 = 10$
$3 \times 1 = 3$	$1 \times 1 = 1$	$3 \div 1 = 3$
$4 \times 1 = 4$	$10 \times 1 = 10$	$9 \div 1 = 9$
$5 \times 1 = 5$	$6 \times 1 = 6$	$1 \div 1 = 1$
$6 \times 1 = 6$	$2 \times 1 = 2$	$4 \div 1 = 4$
$7 \times 1 = 7$	$5 \times 1 = 5$	$5 \div 1 = 5$
$8 \times 1 = 8$	$8 \times 1 = 8$	$8 \div 1 = 8$
$9 \times 1 = 9$	$4 \times 1 = 4$	$2 \div 1 = 2$
$10 \times 1 = 10$	$9 \times 1 = 9$	$6 \div 1 = 6$

0s

× In Order	× Mixed Up
$1 \times 0 = 0$	$3 \times 0 = 0$
$2 \times 0 = 0$	$7 \times 0 = 0$
$3 \times 0 = 0$	$1 \times 0 = 0$
$4 \times 0 = 0$	$10 \times 0 = 0$
$5 \times 0 = 0$	$6 \times 0 = 0$
$6 \times 0 = 0$	$2 \times 0 = 0$
$7 \times 0 = 0$	$5 \times 0 = 0$
$8 \times 0 = 0$	$8 \times 0 = 0$
$9 \times 0 = 0$	$4 \times 0 = 0$
$10 \times 0 = 0$	$9 \times 0 = 0$

Multiply or divide to find the unknown numbers.
Then check your answers at the bottom of this page.

1. $4 \times 1 = \boxed{}$ **2.** $12 \div 3 = \boxed{}$ **3.** $7 * 0 = \boxed{}$

4. $0 / 5 = \boxed{}$ **5.** $4 \cdot \boxed{} = 8$ **6.** $\frac{2}{1} = \boxed{}$

7. $10 \times 1 = \boxed{}$ **8.** $\frac{0}{4} = \boxed{}$ **9.** $1 \times 0 = \boxed{}$

10. $3\overline{)9}$ **11.** $10 \cdot 9 = \boxed{}$ **12.** $0 \div 1 = \boxed{}$

13. $3 * \boxed{} = 3$ **14.** $\frac{8}{1} = \boxed{}$ **15.** $0 \cdot 7 = \boxed{}$

16. $24 / 3 = \boxed{}$ **17.** $1 \div 1 = \boxed{}$ **18.** $10 * 2 = \boxed{}$

19. $\boxed{} \times 3 = 0$ **20.** $3\overline{)18}$ **21.** $1 \times \boxed{} = 4$

22. $\boxed{} \times 5 = 25$ **23.** $6 \cdot 9 = \boxed{}$ **24.** $10 \div 1 = \boxed{}$

1. 4 2. 4 3. 0 4. 0 5. 2 6. 2 7. 10 8. 0 9. 0 10. 3 11. 90 12. 0
13. 1 14. 8 15. 0 16. 8 17. 1 18. 20 19. 0 20. 6 21. 4 22. 5
23. 54 24. 10

Multiply and Divide with 1 and 0

Homework

Study Plan

_____

Homework Helper

Complete.

1. $3 \times (4 \times 2) = \boxed{}$ **2.** $(5 \times 2) \times 8 = \boxed{}$ **3.** $5 \times (0 \times 9) = \boxed{}$

4. $25 \times 1 = \boxed{}$ **5.** $3 \times 9 = 9 \times \boxed{} = \boxed{}$ **6.** $6 \times (3 \times 2) = \boxed{}$

Write an equation and solve the problem.

7. Paul put birthday candles on his brother's cake. He arranged them in an array with 8 rows and 1 column. How many candles did he put on the cake? _____

8. There are 24 people in the brass section of the marching band. They stood in an array with 4 people in each row. How many rows were there?

_____

9. Freya doesn't like peppers, so she grew 0 peppers in her garden. She divided the peppers equally among her 4 cousins. How many peppers did each cousin get? _____

10. Cal had 6 comic books. After he gave 1 comic book to each of his cousins, he had none left. How many cousins does Cal have?

_____

Multiply and Divide with 1 and 0 **83**

Remembering

Solve each problem.

1. Find the area of the large rectangle by finding the area of the two small rectangles and adding them.

   _____

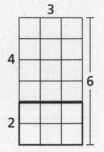

2. Find the area of the large rectangle by multiplying the number of rows by the number of squares units in each row.

   _____

Write an equation and solve the problem.

3. Dwight has 72 pennies in a jar. He takes out 9 pennies. How many pennies are in the jar now?

   _____

4. There are 3 soccer bags. Each bag has 7 soccer balls. How many soccer balls are there in all?

   _____

Multiply or divide to find the unknown numbers.

5. $3\overline{)21}$ 6. $\boxed{} * 10 = 80$ 7. $\dfrac{81}{9} = \boxed{}$

8. $9 \times \boxed{} = 63$ 9. $2 \cdot 6 = \boxed{}$ 10. $\boxed{} \div 5 = 5$

11. **Stretch Your Thinking** Write and solve an equation with the numbers 0 and 9. Then write an equation with the numbers 1 and 9 that has the same answer.

   _____

Homework

Study Plan

_____

Homework Helper

**Read each problem and decide what type of problem it is.
Write the letter from the list below. Then write an equation
and solve the problem.**

a. Array Multiplication

b. Array Division

c. Equal Groups Multiplication

d. Equal Groups Division with an Unknown Group Size

e. Equal Groups Division with an Unknown Multiplier
(number of groups)

1. A farmer collected eggs from the henhouse. He can put 36 eggs in a carton. A carton will hold 6 eggs in a row. How many rows does the egg carton have?

_____

2. The Watertown science contest allowed teams of 5 students to compete. If 45 students entered the contest, how many teams competed?

_____

3. The Happy Feet Shoe Store is having a sale. 10 pairs of shoes are displayed on each row of the sale rack. If the rack has 8 rows, how many pairs of shoes are on sale?

_____

4. Una has 5 goldfish. She bought 2 small water plants for each goldfish. How many plants did she buy?

_____

5. Yolanda made 16 barrettes. She divided the barrettes equally among her 4 friends. How many barrettes did each friend get?

_____

6. Carson has 12 baseball cards to give away. If he gives 3 cards to each friend, how many friends can he give cards to?

_____

Solve and Create Word Problems **85**

Remembering

You can combine multiplications you know to find multiplications you don't know.

1. Find this product: $3 \times 7 =$ _____

2. Find this product: $4 \times 7 =$ _____

3. Use the answers to Exercises 1 and 2 to find this product: $7 \times 7 =$ _____

Write an equation and solve the problem.

Show your work.

4. Susan buys 9 packages of cups. There are 8 cups in each package. How many cups does she buy altogether?

   _____

5. The football team has 30 players. The players line up to exercise with 5 in each row. How many rows are there?

   _____

6. Bill scored 63 points on his video game. He gets 9 points for each level he completes. How many levels did he complete?

   _____

Complete.

7. $4 \times (5 \times 1) = \boxed{}$ 8. $6 \times 9 = 9 \times \boxed{} = \boxed{}$ 9. $(10 \times 1) \times 7 = \boxed{}$

10. $9 \times (5 \times 0) = \boxed{}$ 11. $26 \times 1 = \boxed{}$ 12. $5 \times (3 \times 3) = \boxed{}$

13. **Stretch Your Thinking** Write a word problem using $24 \div 3$. Then solve your problem.

    _____

    _____

Solve and Create Word Problems

Homework

Home Check Sheet 5: 1s and 0s

1s Multiplications	1s Divisions	0s Multiplications
$1 \times 4 = 4$	$10 / 1 = 10$	$4 \times 0 = 0$
$5 \bullet 1 = 5$	$5 \div 1 = 5$	$2 \bullet 0 = 0$
$7 * 1 = 7$	$7 / 1 = 7$	$0 * 8 = 0$
$1 \times 8 = 8$	$9 \div 1 = 9$	$0 \times 5 = 0$
$1 \bullet 6 = 6$	$3 / 1 = 3$	$6 \bullet 0 = 0$
$10 * 1 = 10$	$10 \div 1 = 10$	$0 * 7 = 0$
$1 \times 9 = 9$	$2 / 1 = 2$	$0 \times 2 = 0$
$3 \bullet 1 = 3$	$8 \div 1 = 8$	$0 \bullet 9 = 0$
$1 * 2 = 2$	$6 / 1 = 6$	$10 * 0 = 0$
$1 \times 1 = 1$	$9 / 1 = 9$	$1 \times 0 = 0$
$8 \bullet 1 = 8$	$1 \div 1 = 1$	$0 \bullet 6 = 0$
$1 * 7 = 7$	$5 / 1 = 5$	$9 * 0 = 0$
$1 \times 5 = 5$	$3 \div 1 = 3$	$0 \times 4 = 0$
$6 \bullet 1 = 6$	$4 / 1 = 4$	$3 \bullet 0 = 0$
$1 * 1 = 1$	$2 \div 1 = 2$	$0 * 3 = 0$
$1 \times 10 = 10$	$8 / 1 = 8$	$8 \times 0 = 0$
$9 \bullet 1 = 9$	$4 \div 1 = 4$	$0 \bullet 10 = 0$
$4 * 1 = 4$	$7 \div 1 = 7$	$0 * 1 = 0$
$2 \times 1 = 2$	$1 / 1 = 1$	$5 \times 0 = 0$
$1 \bullet 3 = 3$	$6 \div 1 = 6$	$7 \bullet 0 = 0$

Homework

Home Check Sheet 6: Mixed 3s, 4s, 0s, and 1s

3s, 4s, 0s, 1s Multiplications	3s, 4s, 0s, 1s Multiplications	3s, 4s, 1s Divisions	3s, 4s, 1s Divisions
$5 \times 3 = 15$	$0 \times 5 = 0$	$18 / 3 = 6$	$4 / 1 = 4$
$6 \bullet 4 = 24$	$10 \bullet 1 = 10$	$20 \div 4 = 5$	$21 \div 3 = 7$
$9 * 0 = 0$	$6 * 3 = 18$	$1 / 1 = 1$	$16 / 4 = 4$
$7 \times 1 = 7$	$2 \times 4 = 8$	$21 \div 3 = 7$	$9 \div 1 = 9$
$3 \bullet 3 = 9$	$5 \bullet 0 = 0$	$12 / 4 = 3$	$15 / 3 = 5$
$4 * 7 = 28$	$1 * 2 = 2$	$5 \div 1 = 5$	$8 \div 4 = 2$
$0 \times 10 = 0$	$10 \times 3 = 30$	$15 / 3 = 5$	$5 / 1 = 5$
$1 \bullet 6 = 6$	$5 \bullet 4 = 20$	$24 \div 4 = 6$	$30 \div 3 = 10$
$3 * 4 = 12$	$0 * 8 = 0$	$7 / 1 = 7$	$12 / 4 = 3$
$5 \times 4 = 20$	$6 \times 3 = 18$	$12 / 3 = 4$	$8 / 1 = 8$
$0 \bullet 5 = 0$	$10 \bullet 3 = 30$	$36 \div 4 = 9$	$27 \div 3 = 9$
$9 * 1 = 9$	$9 * 4 = 36$	$6 / 1 = 6$	$40 / 4 = 10$
$2 \times 3 = 6$	$1 \times 0 = 0$	$12 \div 3 = 4$	$4 \div 1 = 4$
$3 \bullet 4 = 12$	$1 \bullet 6 = 6$	$16 / 4 = 4$	$9 / 3 = 3$
$0 * 9 = 0$	$3 * 6 = 18$	$7 \div 1 = 7$	$16 \div 4 = 4$
$1 \times 5 = 5$	$7 \times 4 = 28$	$9 / 3 = 3$	$10 / 1 = 10$
$2 \bullet 3 = 6$	$6 \bullet 0 = 0$	$8 \div 4 = 2$	$9 \div 3 = 3$
$4 * 4 = 16$	$8 * 1 = 8$	$2 \div 1 = 2$	$20 \div 4 = 5$
$9 \times 0 = 0$	$3 \times 9 = 27$	$6 / 3 = 2$	$6 / 1 = 6$
$1 \bullet 1 = 1$	$1 \bullet 4 = 4$	$32 \div 4 = 8$	$24 \div 3 = 8$

Home Check Sheet 6: Mixed 3s, 4s, 0s, and 1s

Homework

Study Plan

_____

Homework Helper

Write an equation and solve the problem.

Show your work.

1. Wendy gave 54 apples to her neighbors.
   She gave away a total of 6 bags of apples.
   She put the same number of apples in each
   bag. How many apples were in each bag?

   _____

2. Dillon had a box of 45 toy trucks. He gave the
   trucks to his brother but kept 9 trucks for himself.
   How many trucks did Dillon give to his brother?

   _____

3. Melissa put 18 stickers in her new sticker album.
   She put them in 6 rows. She put the same number
   of stickers in each row. How many stickers did
   she put in each row?

   _____

4. Yan took photographs at the zoo. He took
   5 photos in each of the 6 animal houses.
   How many photos did he take?

   _____

5. Janie stacked some books at the library.
   She stacked 6 books each in 7 different piles.
   How many books were in the piles?

   _____

Remembering

Multiply or divide to find the unknown numbers.

1. $\dfrac{72}{9} = \boxed{}$
2. $2 * \boxed{} = 14$
3. $40 \div 10 = \boxed{}$

Write an equation and solve the problem.

4. Brian has 0 crackers on his plate and divides them among his 5 friends. How many crackers does each friend get?

_____

Read each problem and decide what type of problem it is. Write the letter from the list below. Then write an equation and solve the problem.

    a. Array Multiplication

    b. Array Division

    c. Equal Groups of Multiplication

    d. Equal Groups Division with Unknown Group Size

    e. Equal Groups Division with an Unknown Multiplier (number of groups)

5. Tiffany is in the bike shop. She counts 27 wheels on all of the tricycles. How many tricycles are in the bike shop?

_____

6. John buys 4 bags of apples. There are 6 apples in each bag. How many apples does John buy?

_____

7. **Stretch Your Thinking** Write a word problem that can be solved using the array shown.

Play Multiplication and Division Games

Name _____   Date _____

Study Plan

Homework Helper

Write an equation and solve the problem.

1. Maili rode her bike 10 miles every day for 5 days. How many miles did she ride?

   _____

2. Leslie gave 72 balloons to children at the fair. After the fair, she had 9 balloons left. How many balloons did Leslie start with?

   _____

3. Tony hung some photographs on one wall in his room. He hung them in 3 rows, with 4 photos in each row. How many photos did Tony hang?

   _____

4. Pepe sent 15 gifts to his family members. He sent an equal amount of gifts to 3 different addresses. How many gifts did he send to each address?

   _____

5. At the Shady Acres Stables, there are 5 horses in each barn. There are 4 barns. How many horses are at Shady Acres?

   _____

6. Sixty students are in the marching band. There are 10 rows of students. How many students are in each row?

   _____

7. Danielle has 35 dolls in her collection. She wants to display them on 5 shelves with the same number of dolls on each shelf. How many dolls should she put on each shelf?

   _____

8. There are 9 players on a baseball team. There are 6 teams in the league. How many baseball players are in the league?

   _____

Remembering

Complete.

1. $5 \times (2 \times 4) = \boxed{}$ **2.** $24 \times 1 = \boxed{}$ **3.** $(9 \times 1) \times 5 = \boxed{}$

Read each problem and decide what type of problem it is. Write the letter from the list below. Then write an equation and solve the problem.

   a. Array Multiplication
   b. Array Division
   c. Equal Groups of Multiplication
   d. Equal Groups Division with Unknown Group Size
   e. Equal Groups Division with an Unknown Multiplier
      (number of groups)

4. Mrs. Patel puts away the crayons. The box holds 63 crayons. She puts 9 in each row. How many rows does the box have?

_____

5. Jackson is planting a garden. He puts 10 corn seeds in a row. If he plants 5 rows of corn seeds, how many corn seeds does he plant?

_____

Write an equation and solve the problem.   *Show your work.*

6. The team has 32 baseball bats in bags. There are 4 bags of bats. Each bag has the same number of bats. How many bats are in each bag?

_____

7. Stretch Your Thinking Each of 5 children is holding up 10 fingers. Explain 3 different ways to find how many fingers are being held up.

_____

_____

_____

Building Fluency with 0s, 1s, 2s, 3s, 4s, 5s, 9s, and 10s

Name _____ **Date** _____

Homework

Find the number.

1. I am 5 more than 6 times 10. What number am I? _____

2. I am 3 less than 8 times 4. What number am I? _____

3. 7 times a number is 21. What is the number? _____

4. 9 times a number is 18. What is the number? _____

5. Use the chart to complete the pictograph.

What is your hobby?

Hobby	Number of Students
Coin Collecting	12
Playing Sports	36
Playing Music	20
Taking Care of Pets	24

Hobbies

Coin Collecting	
Playing Sports	
Playing Music	
Taking Care of Pets	

Each ▮ = 4 third graders

Remembering

Read each problem and decide what type of problem it is. Write the letter from the list below. Then write an equation and solve the problem.

    a. Array Multiplication

    b. Array Division

    c. Equal Groups of Multiplication

    d. Equal Groups Division with Unknown Group Size

    e. Equal Groups Division with an Unknown Multiplier (number of groups)

1. There are 40 toys in 5 boxes. Each box has the same number of toys. How many toys are in each box?

_____

2. Sangeeta has two dogs. She buys 2 collars for each of her dogs. How many collars does she buy?

_____

Write an equation and solve the problem.

Show your work.

3. Darci puts 15 tulips in 5 vases. If she puts the same number of tulips in each vase, how many tulips will be in each vase?

_____

4. Miss Lin has 5 baskets. She puts 4 pears in each basket. How many pears are in the baskets?

_____

5. Steven receives an order for 80 flash drives. He puts the same number of flash drives in 10 boxes. How many flash drives are in each box?

_____

6. Stretch Your Thinking Solve the riddle. I am 6 more than 2 times 9. What number am I? Now make up your own riddle for the number 68.

_____

Homework

Use this chart to practice your 6s count-bys, multiplications, and divisions. Then have your Homework Helper test you.

	× In Order	× Mixed Up	÷ Mixed Up
6s	$1 \times 6 = 6$	$2 \times 6 = 12$	$18 \div 6 = 3$
	$2 \times 6 = 12$	$8 \times 6 = 48$	$60 \div 6 = 10$
	$3 \times 6 = 18$	$5 \times 6 = 30$	$30 \div 6 = 5$
	$4 \times 6 = 24$	$9 \times 6 = 54$	$48 \div 6 = 8$
	$5 \times 6 = 30$	$1 \times 6 = 6$	$12 \div 6 = 2$
	$6 \times 6 = 36$	$7 \times 6 = 42$	$6 \div 6 = 1$
	$7 \times 6 = 42$	$4 \times 6 = 24$	$36 \div 6 = 6$
	$8 \times 6 = 48$	$3 \times 6 = 18$	$24 \div 6 = 4$
	$9 \times 6 = 54$	$10 \times 6 = 60$	$54 \div 6 = 9$
	$10 \times 6 = 60$	$6 \times 6 = 36$	$42 \div 6 = 7$

Name _____ **Date** _____

Homework

Multiply or divide to find the unknown numbers.
Then check your answers at the bottom of this page.

1. $5 \times 5 = \boxed{}$

2. $12 \div 6 = \boxed{}$

3. $7 * 4 = \boxed{}$

4. $42 / 6 = \boxed{}$

5. $6 \bullet \boxed{} = 48$

6. $\frac{6}{1} = \boxed{}$

7. $10 \times 6 = \boxed{}$

8. $9\overline{)27}$ with $\boxed{}$ on top

9. $6 \times 0 = \boxed{}$

10. $20 / 4 = \boxed{}$

11. $6 \bullet 6 = \boxed{}$

12. $18 \div 3 = \boxed{}$

13. $9 * \boxed{} = 54$

14. $\frac{60}{6} = \boxed{}$

15. $2 \bullet 7 = \boxed{}$

16. $16 / 4 = \boxed{}$

17. $6 \div 6 = \boxed{}$

18. $6 * 7 = \boxed{}$

19. $\boxed{} \times 7 = 0$

20. $9\overline{)45}$ with $\boxed{}$ on top

21. $1 \times \boxed{} = 10$

1. 25 2. 2 3. 28 4. 7 5. 8 6. 6 7. 60 8. 3 9. 0 10. 5 11. 36
12. 6 13. 6 14. 10 15. 14 16. 4 17. 1 18. 42 19. 0 20. 5 21. 10

Multiply and Divide with 6

Homework

Study Plan
Homework Helper

Find the unknown number.

1. $6 \times \boxed{} = 54$ **2.** $\boxed{} \times 7 = 42$ **3.** $6 \times \boxed{} = 18$

4. $\boxed{} \div 6 = 8$ **5.** $36 \div \boxed{} = 6$ **6.** $\boxed{} \div 6 = 5$

Solve each problem.

7. Tim has 6 cats and 4 birds for pets. How many pets does Tim have?

_____

8. Six friends decided to go to the movies. If each person spent $9 to buy tickets, what was the total amount of money spent on tickets?

_____

9. Jing charges $7 for each lawn she mows. Last week, she mowed 6 lawns. How much money did she earn from mowing lawns?

_____

10. The grocery store is having a sale on six-packs of bottled water. Raj bought 48 bottles in all. How many six-packs did he buy?

_____

11. The desks in Ms. Toledo's classroom are arranged in 6 equal rows. There are 30 desks in the room. How many desks are in each row?

_____

12. Kendall arranged her pennies in an array with 6 rows and 6 columns. How many pennies does Kendall have?

_____

Remembering

Multiply or divide to find the unknown numbers.

1. $35 \div 5 = \boxed{}$ **2.** $2 * \boxed{} = 16$ **3.** $5\overline{)10} = \boxed{}$

Write an equation and solve the problem.

4. Olivia arranges strawberries on her plate. She arranges them in 5 rows and 1 column. How many strawberries does she arrange on her plate?

_____

Read each problem and decide what type of problem it is. Write the letter from the list below. Then write an equation and solve the problem.

    a. Array Multiplication

    b. Array Division

    c. Equal Groups of Multiplication

    d. Equal Groups Division with Unknown Group Size

    e. Equal Groups Division with an Unknown Multiplier (number of groups)

5. The store owner has 32 new CDs. She divides them equally among 4 shelves. How many CDs are on each shelf?

_____

6. Evan has 5 notebooks. There are 4 dividers in each notebook. How many dividers are in the notebooks?

_____

7. Stretch Your Thinking Anna has 12 baseballs to display in her store window. She wants to display them in equal groups. List all the ways Anna can display the baseballs in which each group has the same number of baseballs.

_____

_____

_____

     Multiply and Divide with 6

Homework

Name _____ Date _____

Home Study Sheet C

6s

Count-bys	Mixed Up ×	Mixed Up ÷
$1 \times 6 = 6$	$10 \times 6 = 60$	$54 \div 6 = 9$
$2 \times 6 = 12$	$8 \times 6 = 48$	$30 \div 6 = 5$
$3 \times 6 = 18$	$2 \times 6 = 12$	$12 \div 6 = 2$
$4 \times 6 = 24$	$6 \times 6 = 36$	$60 \div 6 = 10$
$5 \times 6 = 30$	$4 \times 6 = 24$	$48 \div 6 = 8$
$6 \times 6 = 36$	$1 \times 6 = 6$	$36 \div 6 = 6$
$7 \times 6 = 42$	$9 \times 6 = 54$	$6 \div 6 = 1$
$8 \times 6 = 48$	$3 \times 6 = 18$	$42 \div 6 = 7$
$9 \times 6 = 54$	$7 \times 6 = 42$	$18 \div 6 = 3$
$10 \times 6 = 60$	$5 \times 6 = 30$	$24 \div 6 = 4$

7s

Count-bys	Mixed Up ×	Mixed Up ÷
$1 \times 7 = 7$	$6 \times 7 = 42$	$70 \div 7 = 10$
$2 \times 7 = 14$	$8 \times 7 = 56$	$14 \div 7 = 2$
$3 \times 7 = 21$	$5 \times 7 = 35$	$28 \div 7 = 4$
$4 \times 7 = 28$	$9 \times 7 = 63$	$56 \div 7 = 8$
$5 \times 7 = 35$	$4 \times 7 = 28$	$42 \div 7 = 6$
$6 \times 7 = 42$	$10 \times 7 = 70$	$63 \div 7 = 9$
$7 \times 7 = 49$	$3 \times 7 = 21$	$21 \div 7 = 3$
$8 \times 7 = 56$	$1 \times 7 = 7$	$49 \div 7 = 7$
$9 \times 7 = 63$	$7 \times 7 = 49$	$7 \div 7 = 1$
$10 \times 7 = 70$	$2 \times 7 = 14$	$35 \div 7 = 5$

8s

Count-bys	Mixed Up ×	Mixed Up ÷
$1 \times 8 = 8$	$6 \times 8 = 48$	$16 \div 8 = 2$
$2 \times 8 = 16$	$10 \times 8 = 80$	$40 \div 8 = 5$
$3 \times 8 = 24$	$7 \times 8 = 56$	$72 \div 8 = 9$
$4 \times 8 = 32$	$2 \times 8 = 16$	$32 \div 8 = 4$
$5 \times 8 = 40$	$4 \times 8 = 32$	$8 \div 8 = 1$
$6 \times 8 = 48$	$8 \times 8 = 64$	$80 \div 8 = 10$
$7 \times 8 = 56$	$5 \times 8 = 40$	$64 \div 8 = 8$
$8 \times 8 = 64$	$10 \times 8 = 80$	$24 \div 8 = 3$
$9 \times 8 = 72$	$3 \times 8 = 24$	$56 \div 8 = 7$
$10 \times 8 = 80$	$1 \times 8 = 8$	$48 \div 8 = 6$

squares

Count-bys	Mixed Up ×	Mixed Up ÷
$1 \times 1 = 1$	$3 \times 3 = 9$	$25 \div 5 = 5$
$2 \times 2 = 4$	$9 \times 9 = 81$	$4 \div 2 = 2$
$3 \times 3 = 9$	$4 \times 4 = 16$	$81 \div 9 = 9$
$4 \times 4 = 16$	$6 \times 6 = 36$	$9 \div 3 = 3$
$5 \times 5 = 25$	$2 \times 2 = 4$	$36 \div 6 = 6$
$6 \times 6 = 36$	$7 \times 7 = 49$	$100 \div 10 = 10$
$7 \times 7 = 49$	$10 \times 10 = 100$	$16 \div 4 = 4$
$8 \times 8 = 64$	$1 \times 1 = 1$	$49 \div 7 = 7$
$9 \times 9 = 81$	$5 \times 5 = 25$	$1 \div 1 = 1$
$10 \times 10 = 100$	$8 \times 8 = 64$	$64 \div 8 = 8$

Homework

Multiply or divide to find the unknown numbers.
Then check your answers at the bottom of this page.

1. $6 \times 6 = \boxed{}$

2. $20 \div 4 = \boxed{}$

3. $9 * 9 = \boxed{}$

4. $32 / 4 = \boxed{}$

5. $9 \bullet \boxed{} = 54$

6. $\frac{30}{10} = \boxed{}$

7. $5 \times 0 = \boxed{}$

8. $\frac{48}{6} = \boxed{}$

9. $3 \times 6 = \boxed{}$

10. $6\overline{)30}$

11. $8 \bullet 4 = \boxed{}$

12. $12 \div 6 = \boxed{}$

13. $6 * \boxed{} = 42$

14. $\frac{6}{6} = \boxed{}$

15. $3 \bullet 4 = \boxed{}$

16. $15 / 5 = \boxed{}$

17. $10 \div 10 = \boxed{}$

18. $2 * 7 = \boxed{}$

19. $\boxed{} \times 2 = 10$

20. $6\overline{)18}$

21. $10 \times \boxed{} = 70$

1. 36 2. 5 3. 81 4. 8 5. 6 6. 3 7. 0 8. 8 9. 18 10. 5 11. 32
12. 2 13. 7 14. 1 15. 12 16. 3 17. 1 18. 14 19. 5 20. 3 21. 7

Homework

Name _____   **Date** _____

Study Plan

_____

Homework Helper

Complete each Unknown Number puzzle.

1.

×			6
9	36		
2			
	12	9	

2.

×	7		6
	28		24
6		30	
	56		48

3.

×			4
5		30	
7	56	42	
			12

Solve each problem. Label your answers with the correct units.

4. Raul built a rectangular tabletop with a length of 3 feet and a width of 6 feet. What is the area of the tabletop?

_____

5. Li Fong covered the rectangular floor of his tree house with 48 square feet of carpeting. If one side of the floor has a length of 6 feet, what is the length of the adjacent side?

_____

6. Frances wants to paint a rectangular wall that has a width of 8 feet and a height of 9 feet. She has a quart of paint that will cover 85 square feet. What is the area of the wall? Does Frances have enough paint?

_____

7. Willis cut out a paper rectangle with an area of 42 square centimeters. If one side has a length of 6 centimeters, what is the length of the adjacent side?

_____

Remembering

Complete.

1. $3 \times (5 \times 1) = \boxed{}$ **2.** $(2 \times 5) \times 3 = \boxed{}$ **3.** $(0 \times 4) \times 9 = \boxed{}$

4. $22 \times 1 = \boxed{}$ **5.** $4 \times 7 = 7 \times \boxed{} = \boxed{}$ **6.** $(3 \times 3) \times 6 = \boxed{}$

Read the problem and decide what type of problem it is. Write the letter from the list below. Then write an equation and solve the problem.

> **a.** Array Multiplication
> **b.** Array Division
> **c.** Equal Groups of Multiplication
> **d.** Equal Division with Unknown Group Size
> **e.** Equal Division with an Unknown Multiplier (number of groups)

7. Andrew has 18 invitations to write. If he writes 3 invitations a day, how many days will it take him to finish?

_____

Solve each problem.

8. Brian buys 6 video games. They cost $10 each. How much does he spend on the video games?

9. Sharon plants 48 rose bushes. Each row has 6 rose bushes. How many rows of rose bushes does Sharon plant?

10. Stretch Your Thinking Ming's rug has a length that is 2 times its width. The area of the rug is 8 square feet. What is the length and width of Ming's rug?

Homework

Use this chart to practice your 8s count-bys, multiplications, and divisions. Then have your Homework Helper test you.

8s	× In Order	× Mixed Up	÷ Mixed Up
	$1 \times 8 = 8$	$3 \times 8 = 24$	$40 \div 8 = 5$
	$2 \times 8 = 16$	$9 \times 8 = 72$	$56 \div 8 = 7$
	$3 \times 8 = 24$	$6 \times 8 = 48$	$24 \div 8 = 3$
	$4 \times 8 = 32$	$4 \times 8 = 32$	$72 \div 8 = 9$
	$5 \times 8 = 40$	$2 \times 8 = 16$	$8 \div 8 = 1$
	$6 \times 8 = 48$	$8 \times 8 = 64$	$48 \div 8 = 6$
	$7 \times 8 = 56$	$1 \times 8 = 8$	$32 \div 8 = 4$
	$8 \times 8 = 64$	$5 \times 8 = 40$	$64 \div 8 = 8$
	$9 \times 8 = 72$	$10 \times 8 = 80$	$16 \div 8 = 2$
	$10 \times 8 = 80$	$7 \times 8 = 56$	$80 \div 8 = 10$

Multiply and Divide with 8 **103**

Homework

Home Check Sheet 7: 6s and 8s

6s Multiplications	6s Divisions	8s Multiplications	8s Divisions
$10 \times 6 = 60$	$24 / 6 = 4$	$2 \times 8 = 16$	$72 / 8 = 9$
$6 \cdot 4 = 24$	$48 \div 6 = 8$	$8 \cdot 10 = 80$	$16 \div 8 = 2$
$6 * 7 = 42$	$60 / 6 = 10$	$3 * 8 = 24$	$40 / 8 = 5$
$2 \times 6 = 12$	$12 \div 6 = 2$	$9 \times 8 = 72$	$8 \div 8 = 1$
$6 \cdot 5 = 30$	$42 / 6 = 7$	$8 \cdot 4 = 32$	$80 / 8 = 10$
$6 * 8 = 48$	$30 \div 6 = 5$	$8 * 7 = 56$	$48 \div 8 = 6$
$9 \times 6 = 54$	$6 / 6 = 1$	$5 \times 8 = 40$	$56 / 8 = 7$
$6 \cdot 1 = 6$	$18 \div 6 = 3$	$8 \cdot 6 = 48$	$24 \div 8 = 3$
$6 * 6 = 36$	$54 / 6 = 9$	$1 * 8 = 8$	$64 / 8 = 8$
$6 \times 3 = 18$	$36 / 6 = 6$	$8 \times 8 = 64$	$32 / 8 = 4$
$6 \cdot 6 = 36$	$48 \div 6 = 8$	$4 \cdot 8 = 32$	$80 \div 8 = 10$
$5 * 6 = 30$	$12 / 6 = 2$	$6 * 8 = 48$	$56 / 8 = 7$
$6 \times 2 = 12$	$24 \div 6 = 4$	$8 \times 3 = 24$	$8 \div 8 = 1$
$4 \cdot 6 = 24$	$60 / 6 = 10$	$7 \cdot 8 = 56$	$24 / 8 = 3$
$6 * 9 = 54$	$6 \div 6 = 1$	$8 * 2 = 16$	$64 \div 8 = 8$
$8 \times 6 = 48$	$42 / 6 = 7$	$8 \times 9 = 72$	$16 / 8 = 2$
$7 \cdot 6 = 42$	$18 \div 6 = 3$	$8 \cdot 1 = 8$	$72 \div 8 = 9$
$6 * 10 = 60$	$36 \div 6 = 6$	$8 * 8 = 64$	$32 \div 8 = 4$
$1 \times 6 = 6$	$30 / 6 = 5$	$10 \times 8 = 80$	$40 / 8 = 5$
$4 \cdot 6 = 24$	$54 \div 6 = 9$	$5 \cdot 8 = 40$	$48 \div 8 = 6$

Study Plan
Homework Helper

Find the unknown number for each Fast-Array Drawing.

1.

9
oooooooooo
o
o
o
8 o ☐
o
o
o

2.

☐
2 o⎯⎯⎯⎯⎯⎯⎯
18

3.

7
o ooooooo
☐ o
o 35
o

Write an equation and solve the problem.

4. Tyrone planted 3 seeds every day for 8 days. How many seeds did Tyrone plant?

_____

5. There are 6 players on a volleyball team. How many players are in a game with 2 teams?

_____

6. Joseph gave his 6 nephews $48 for helping him clean out the garage. The boys divided the money equally. How much money did each boy get?

_____

7. Miki has 3 planting boxes for her flowers. Each box is 4 feet wide and 8 feet long. How much area for planting flowers does Miki have altogether?

_____

Name _____   **Date** _____

Remembering

Write an equation and solve the problem.   *Show your work.*

1. There are 0 tickets available. There are 6 people in line to purchase tickets. How many tickets did they purchase?

_____

Read each problem and decide what type of problem it is. Write the letter from the list below. Then write an equation and solve the problem.

   a. Array Multiplication

   b. Array Division

   c. Equal Groups of Multiplication

   d. Equal Groups Division with Unknown Group Size

   e. Equal Groups Division with an Unknown Multiplier (number of groups)

2. Owen orders 9 boxes of hammers for the hardware store. Each box has 10 hammers. How many hammers does Owen order?

_____

3. Tameka has 12 granola bars for the bake sale. She puts 4 granola bars on each plate. How many plates does she fill?

_____

Complete each Unknown Number puzzle.

4.

×		5
	12	36
6		
2	6	

5.

×	2		6
		45	
3		27	
		63	42

6.

×		7	3
	20		15
9		63	
	24		

7. **Stretch Your Thinking** A pizza parlor has 8 different toppings and 3 different cheeses to choose from on the menu. How many pizza combinations are possible if each pizza has 1 topping and 1 cheese?

_____

    Multiply and Divide with 8

Name _____ **Date** _____

Study Plan

_____

Homework Helper

Solve. Then circle what type it is and what operation you used.

1. The area of a photograph is 15 square inches. If the width of the photograph is 3 inches, what is its length?

_____

array   equal groups   area

multiplication   division

2. Mrs. Divita divided 64 beetles equally among the 8 students in the science club. How many beetles did each student receive?

_____

array   equal groups   area

multiplication   division

3. Write your own problem that is the same type as Problem 1.

_____

_____

_____

4. Write your own problem that is the same type as Problem 2.

_____

_____

_____

Find the unknown number for each Fast-Array Drawing.

5.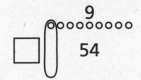
9
54

6.
4
7

7.
6   36

Name _____   **Date** _____

Remembering

Write an equation and solve the problem.   *Show your work.*

1. Lucy puts 54 pictures in her photo album. She puts 9 photos on each page. How many pages does she fill?

   _____

2. Chris sets up 8 chairs in each row. He sets up 7 rows. How many chairs does Chris set up?

   _____

3. Trina places 4 peaches in each gift basket. She puts together 9 gift baskets to sell in her store. How many peaches does Trina use?

   _____

4. Jorge has 15 science fair awards. He wants to display the same number of awards among 3 shelves. How many awards should he put on each shelf?

   _____

Find the unknown number for each Fast Array Drawing.

5.

6.

7.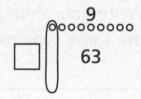

8. **Stretch Your Thinking** Write a real world problem and equation using $t = 5$.

   _____

   _____

   _____

Homework

Use this chart to practice your 7s count-bys, multiplications, and divisions. Then have your Homework Helper test you.

	× In Order	× Mixed Up	÷ Mixed Up
7s	$1 \times 7 = 7$	$5 \times 7 = 35$	$56 \div 7 = 8$
	$2 \times 7 = 14$	$1 \times 7 = 7$	$42 \div 7 = 6$
	$3 \times 7 = 21$	$10 \times 7 = 70$	$14 \div 7 = 2$
	$4 \times 7 = 28$	$2 \times 7 = 14$	$7 \div 7 = 1$
	$5 \times 7 = 35$	$9 \times 7 = 63$	$70 \div 7 = 10$
	$6 \times 7 = 42$	$3 \times 7 = 21$	$49 \div 7 = 7$
	$7 \times 7 = 49$	$8 \times 7 = 56$	$21 \div 7 = 3$
	$8 \times 7 = 56$	$4 \times 7 = 28$	$35 \div 7 = 5$
	$9 \times 7 = 63$	$7 \times 7 = 49$	$63 \div 7 = 9$
	$10 \times 7 = 70$	$6 \times 7 = 42$	$28 \div 7 = 4$

Homework

Name

Date

Multiply or divide to find the unknown numbers. Then check your answers at the bottom of this page.

1. $7 \times 7 = \boxed{}$

2. $\dfrac{64}{8} = \boxed{}$

3. $5 \times 5 = \boxed{}$

4. $28 / 7 = \boxed{}$

5. $9 \bullet \boxed{} = 27$

6. $\dfrac{48}{6} = \boxed{}$

7. $\boxed{} \times 9 = 63$

8. $7\overline{)56}$ with $\boxed{}$ on top

9. $10 \times \boxed{} = 30$

10. $8 \times 5 = \boxed{}$

11. $21 \div 3 = \boxed{}$

12. $9 * 2 = \boxed{}$

13. $30 / 6 = \boxed{}$

14. $8 \bullet 5 = \boxed{}$

15. $24 \div 3 = \boxed{}$

16. $3\overline{)21}$ with $\boxed{}$ on top

17. $90 \div 9 = \boxed{}$

18. $2 * 7 = \boxed{}$

19. $6 * \boxed{} = 42$

20. $\dfrac{10}{2} = \boxed{}$

21. $3 \bullet 9 = \boxed{}$

1. 49 2. 8 3. 25 4. 4 5. 3 6. 8 7. 7 8. 8 9. 3 10. 40 11. 7
12. 18 13. 5 14. 40 15. 8 16. 7 17. 10 18. 14 19. 7 20. 5 21. 27

Multiply and Divide with 7

Homework

Study Plan

_____

Homework Helper

Find the unknown number for each Fast-Array Drawing.

1. ☐ 7
      21

2. 9
   5 ☐

3. ☐
   5 35

4. 9
   8 ☐

5. ☐ 9
      45

6. ☐
   7 49

Solve. Label your answers.

7. Rachel plans to fence in an area 7 meters long by 7 meters wide for her dog to run in. How much area will her dog have to run in?

_____

8. Shondra has 21 tropical fish. If she divides them evenly among 3 tanks, how many fish will be in each tank?

_____

9. Write a word problem that involves an array and multiplication. Write your problem on a separate sheet of paper for your teacher to collect.

Multiply and Divide with 7 **111**

Remembering

Write an equation and solve the problem. *Show your work.*

1. Sara picks 48 apples. She puts 6 apples in each basket. How many baskets does she fill?

_____

2. Mrs. Lin places 5 pencils at each table in the classroom. There are 7 tables in the classroom. How many pencils does Mrs. Lin place on the tables?

_____

3. Gibson has an assignment to read 8 pages in his reading book. It takes him 2 minutes to read each page. How many minutes will it take him to finish the reading assignment?

_____

4. There are 4 paper towel rolls in each package. There are 7 packages of paper towel rolls on the shelf. How many paper towel rolls are on the shelf?

_____

Solve. Then circle what type it is and what operation you used.

5. The area of the paper is 80 square inches. If the width of the paper is 8 inches, what is its length?

_____

array   equal groups   area

multiplication   division

6. The desks are in 6 rows, with 5 desks in each row. How many desks are in the classroom?

_____

array   equal groups   area

multiplication   division

7. **Stretch Your Thinking** Write a word problem using 7 groups. Solve your problem.

_____

_____

Multiply and Divide with 7

Homework

Home Check Sheet 8: 7s and Squares

7s Multiplications	7s Divisions	Squares Multiplications	Squares Divisions
$4 \times 7 = 28$	$14 / 7 = 2$	$8 \times 8 = 64$	$81 / 9 = 9$
$7 \cdot 2 = 14$	$28 \div 7 = 4$	$10 \cdot 10 = 100$	$4 \div 2 = 2$
$7 * 8 = 56$	$70 / 7 = 10$	$3 * 3 = 9$	$25 / 5 = 5$
$7 \times 7 = 49$	$56 \div 7 = 8$	$9 \times 9 = 81$	$1 \div 1 = 1$
$7 \cdot 1 = 7$	$42 / 7 = 6$	$4 \cdot 4 = 16$	$100 / 10 = 10$
$7 * 10 = 70$	$63 \div 7 = 9$	$7 * 7 = 49$	$36 \div 6 = 6$
$3 \times 7 = 21$	$7 / 7 = 1$	$5 \times 5 = 25$	$49 / 7 = 7$
$7 \cdot 6 = 42$	$49 \div 7 = 7$	$6 \cdot 6 = 36$	$9 \div 3 = 3$
$5 * 7 = 35$	$21 / 7 = 3$	$1 * 1 = 1$	$64 / 8 = 8$
$7 \times 9 = 63$	$35 / 7 = 5$	$5 * 5 = 25$	$16 / 4 = 4$
$7 \cdot 4 = 28$	$7 \div 7 = 1$	$1 \cdot 1 = 1$	$100 \div 10 = 10$
$9 * 7 = 63$	$63 / 7 = 9$	$3 \cdot 3 = 9$	$49 / 7 = 7$
$2 \times 7 = 14$	$14 \div 7 = 2$	$10 \times 10 = 100$	$1 \div 1 = 1$
$7 \cdot 5 = 35$	$70 / 7 = 10$	$4 \times 4 = 16$	$9 / 3 = 3$
$8 * 7 = 56$	$21 \div 7 = 3$	$9 * 9 = 81$	$64 \div 8 = 8$
$7 \times 3 = 21$	$49 / 7 = 7$	$2 \times 2 = 4$	$4 / 2 = 2$
$6 \cdot 7 = 42$	$28 \div 7 = 4$	$6 * 6 = 36$	$81 \div 9 = 9$
$10 * 7 = 70$	$56 \div 7 = 8$	$7 \times 7 = 49$	$16 \div 4 = 4$
$1 \times 7 = 7$	$35 / 7 = 5$	$5 \cdot 5 = 25$	$25 / 5 = 5$
$7 \cdot 7 = 49$	$42 \div 7 = 6$	$8 \cdot 8 = 64$	$36 \div 6 = 6$

Homework

Multiply or divide to find the unknown numbers. Then check your answers at the bottom of this page.

1. $\boxed{} \times 6 = 48$

2. $56 \div 7 = \boxed{}$

3. $10 \times \boxed{} = 90$

4. $64 / 8 = \boxed{}$

5. $9 \bullet \boxed{} = 63$

6. $\dfrac{25}{5} = \boxed{}$

7. $8 \times 9 = \boxed{}$

8. $9\overline{)36}$ with $\boxed{}$

9. $7 * 7 = \boxed{}$

10. $6 * \boxed{} = 36$

11. $\dfrac{32}{4} = \boxed{}$

12. $3 \bullet 3 = \boxed{}$

13. $30 / 6 = \boxed{}$

14. $16 \div 4 = \boxed{}$

15. $8 * 5 = \boxed{}$

16. $6 \times 4 = \boxed{}$

17. $\dfrac{81}{9} = \boxed{}$

18. $5 \times 7 = \boxed{}$

19. $60 / 6 = \boxed{}$

20. $7 \bullet 8 = \boxed{}$

21. $42 \div 7 = \boxed{}$

22. $6\overline{)54}$ with $\boxed{}$

23. $32 \div 8 = \boxed{}$

24. $9 * 9 = \boxed{}$

23. 4   24. 81
13. 5   14. 4   15. 40   16. 24   17. 9   18. 35   19. 10   20. 56   21. 6   22. 9
1. 8   2. 8   3. 9   4. 8   5. 7   6. 5   7. 72   8. 4   9. 49   10. 6   11. 8   12. 9

Square Numbers

Name _____ Date _____

Study Plan
Homework Helper

Write a multiplication equation for each square array.

1.

_____

2.

_____

3.

_____

Solve.

4. Julia used 1 foot square stone tiles to make a patio. She laid the tiles in a square, 7 tiles wide by 7 tiles long. What is the area of Julia's new patio?

_____

5. Sal brought 2 dozen apples to a science club meeting. He divided the apples equally among the 8 people there. How many apples did he give each person?

_____

6. Lehie has 21 crystals in her collection. Her brother Tomer has 7 crystals. How many more crystals does Lehie have than Tomer?

_____

7. Emmanuel collected 49 leaves last week. He collected the same number of leaves each day. How many leaves did he collect on Monday?

_____

Complete.

8.

×	6	4	
	24		32

9.

×		4	
9	45		81

10.

×	8		3
8		56	

Name _____ **Date** _____

Remembering

Write an equation and solve the problem.   *Show your work.*

1. There are 5 birch trees in each row at the nursery. There are 9 rows of birch trees. How many birch trees are in the nursery?

_____

2. There are 54 dictionaries in the library. There are 6 shelves of dictionaries. Each shelf has the same number of dictionaries. How many dictionaries are on each shelf?

_____

3. Samuel orders 6 boxes of robots for his store. There are 4 robots in each box. How many robots does Samuel order?

4. A pet store has 24 tiger fish in 3 aquariums. Each aquarium has the same number of tiger fish. How many tiger fish are in each aquarium?

_____   _____

Find the unknown number for each Fast Array Drawing.

5.

6.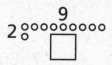

7.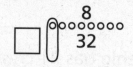

8. **Stretch Your Thinking** Explain two different squares that can be made using the number 9.

_____

Square Numbers

2-7

Homework

Home Check Sheet 9: 6s, 7s, and 8s

6s, 7s, and 8s Multiplications	6s, 7s, and 8s Multiplications	6s, 7s, and 8s Divisions	6s, 7s, and 8s Divisions
$1 \times 6 = 6$	$0 \times 8 = 0$	$24 / 6 = 4$	$54 / 6 = 9$
$6 \cdot 7 = 42$	$6 \cdot 2 = 12$	$21 \div 7 = 3$	$24 \div 8 = 3$
$3 * 8 = 24$	$4 * 7 = 28$	$16 / 8 = 2$	$14 / 7 = 2$
$6 \times 2 = 12$	$8 \times 3 = 24$	$24 \div 8 = 3$	$32 \div 8 = 4$
$7 \cdot 5 = 35$	$5 \cdot 6 = 30$	$14 / 7 = 2$	$18 / 6 = 3$
$8 * 4 = 32$	$7 * 2 = 14$	$30 \div 6 = 5$	$56 \div 7 = 8$
$6 \times 6 = 36$	$3 \times 8 = 24$	$35 / 7 = 5$	$40 / 8 = 5$
$8 \cdot 7 = 56$	$6 \cdot 4 = 24$	$24 \div 8 = 3$	$35 \div 7 = 5$
$9 * 8 = 72$	$0 * 7 = 0$	$18 / 6 = 3$	$12 / 6 = 2$
$6 \times 10 = 60$	$8 \times 1 = 8$	$12 / 6 = 2$	$21 / 7 = 3$
$7 \cdot 1 = 7$	$8 \cdot 6 = 48$	$42 \div 7 = 6$	$16 \div 8 = 2$
$8 * 3 = 24$	$7 * 9 = 63$	$56 / 8 = 7$	$42 / 6 = 7$
$5 \times 6 = 30$	$10 \times 8 = 80$	$49 \div 7 = 7$	$80 \div 8 = 10$
$4 \cdot 7 = 28$	$6 \cdot 10 = 60$	$16 / 8 = 2$	$36 / 6 = 6$
$2 * 8 = 16$	$3 * 7 = 21$	$60 \div 6 = 10$	$7 \div 7 = 1$
$7 \times 7 = 49$	$8 \times 4 = 32$	$54 / 6 = 9$	$64 / 8 = 8$
$7 \cdot 6 = 42$	$6 \cdot 5 = 30$	$8 \div 8 = 1$	$24 \div 6 = 4$
$8 * 8 = 64$	$7 * 4 = 28$	$28 \div 7 = 4$	$21 \div 7 = 3$
$9 \times 6 = 54$	$8 \times 8 = 64$	$72 / 8 = 9$	$49 / 7 = 7$
$10 \cdot 7 = 70$	$6 \cdot 9 = 54$	$56 \div 7 = 8$	$24 \div 8 = 3$

Homework

Home Check Sheet 10: 0s–10s

0s–10s Multiplications	0s–10s Multiplications	0s–10s Divisions	0s–10s Divisions
$9 \times 0 = 0$	$9 \times 4 = 36$	$9 / 1 = 9$	$90 / 10 = 9$
$1 \cdot 1 = 1$	$5 \cdot 9 = 45$	$12 \div 3 = 4$	$64 \div 8 = 8$
$2 * 3 = 6$	$6 * 10 = 60$	$14 / 2 = 7$	$15 / 5 = 3$
$1 \times 3 = 3$	$7 \times 3 = 21$	$20 \div 4 = 5$	$12 \div 6 = 2$
$5 \cdot 4 = 20$	$5 \cdot 3 = 15$	$10 / 5 = 2$	$14 / 7 = 2$
$7 * 5 = 35$	$4 * 1 = 4$	$48 \div 8 = 6$	$45 \div 9 = 5$
$6 \times 9 = 54$	$7 \times 5 = 35$	$35 / 7 = 5$	$8 / 1 = 8$
$4 \cdot 7 = 28$	$6 \cdot 3 = 18$	$60 \div 6 = 10$	$30 \div 3 = 10$
$1 * 8 = 8$	$8 * 7 = 56$	$81 / 9 = 9$	$16 / 4 = 4$
$9 \times 8 = 72$	$5 \times 8 = 40$	$20 / 10 = 2$	$8 / 2 = 4$
$2 \cdot 10 = 20$	$9 \cdot 9 = 81$	$16 \div 2 = 8$	$80 \div 10 = 8$
$0 * 7 = 0$	$9 * 10 = 90$	$30 / 5 = 6$	$36 / 4 = 9$
$4 \times 1 = 4$	$0 \times 0 = 0$	$49 \div 7 = 7$	$25 \div 5 = 5$
$2 \cdot 4 = 8$	$1 \cdot 0 = 0$	$60 / 6 = 10$	$42 / 7 = 6$
$10 * 3 = 30$	$1 * 6 = 6$	$30 \div 3 = 10$	$36 \div 6 = 6$
$8 \times 4 = 32$	$7 \times 2 = 14$	$8 / 1 = 8$	$90 / 9 = 10$
$5 \cdot 8 = 40$	$6 \cdot 3 = 18$	$16 \div 4 = 4$	$24 \div 8 = 3$
$4 * 6 = 24$	$4 * 5 = 20$	$16 \div 8 = 2$	$6 \div 2 = 3$
$7 \times 6 = 42$	$6 \times 6 = 36$	$40 / 10 = 4$	$9 / 3 = 3$
$1 \cdot 8 = 8$	$10 \cdot 7 = 70$	$36 \div 9 = 4$	$1 \div 1 = 1$

Name _____ **Date** _____

Homework

Study Plan
Homework Helper

Solve.

1. Sarah's chickens laid 3 dozen eggs over the weekend. She divided them equally into cartons to give away to her 6 closest neighbors. How many eggs did she put in each carton?

   _____

2. Latisha needs 60 square feet of cloth. She has a rectangular piece of cloth that measures 3 feet by 9 feet, and a square piece that measures 5 feet on a side. Does she have enough cloth? If not, how much more does she need?

   _____

3. Lucy has 6 sheets of stickers. Each sheet has 8 stickers. How many stickers does Lucy have?

   _____

4. A park ranger led 3 groups of hikers. There were 7 people in each group. How many hikers did she lead?

   _____

Find the unknown number for each Fast-Array.

5.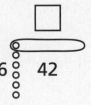

6.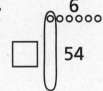

7.

Name _____ **Date** _____

Remembering

Write an equation and solve the problem.

1. Adam has 60 plates. He places 10 plates on each table. How many tables does Adam place plates on?

_____

2. Hailey draws 35 leaves on her tree. She draws 5 leaves on each branch. How many branches are on her tree?

_____

Find the unknown number for each Fast Array Drawing.

3.

4.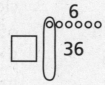

5.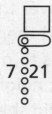

Write a multiplication equation for each array.

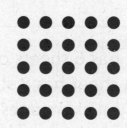

6. _____ 7. _____ 8. _____

9. **Stretch Your Thinking** Draw a picture to show 7×7.

Practice with 6s, 7s, and 8s

Homework

Study Plan

_____

Homework Helper

Write an equation to solve the problem.

1. Maria created artwork by placing all of her seashells in 4 rows on a wall. In each row, she arranged 8 seashells. How many seashells did Maria collect in all?

_____

2. Arturo collected 18 seashells. He wants to divide the seashells evenly among his 3 best friends. How many seashells will each friend receive?

_____

Use the pictograph and key to solve.

Katie planted pumpkins in the spring. Now she is selling them. This pictograph shows how many pumpkins she sold this weekend.

Friday	🎃 🎃 🎃 🎃
Saturday	🎃 🎃 🎃 🎃 🎃 🎃 🎃
Sunday	🎃 🎃 🎃

Key: 🎃 = 6 pumpkins

3. How many pumpkins did Katie sell on Friday?

_____

4. How many more pumpkins did she sell on Saturday than on Friday?

_____

5. How many pumpkins did Katie sell this weekend?

_____

Remembering

Write an equation and solve the problem.

1. The fitness instructor puts the class into 10 rows. There are 6 people in each row. How many people are in the class?

_____

2. Jared has 40 stars. He puts the same number of stars in each of 5 rows. How many stars are in each row?

_____

Write a multiplication equation for each array.

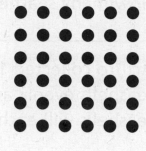

3. _____ **4.** _____ **5.** _____

Solve.

6. Amanda has 8 boxes of markers. Each box has 7 markers. How many markers in all are in the boxes?

_____

7. Alex has 7 shirts. He sews 6 buttons on each shirt. How many buttons does Alex sew on the shirts?

_____

8. Stretch Your Thinking Write a word problem with 16 for the product.

_____

_____

_____

Building Fluency with 0s–10s

Name _____ Date _____

Study Plan

_____

Homework Helper

Write an equation and solve the problem.

1. Robert planted 7 trees behind Westwood School. He planted 6 times as many trees in front of the school. How many trees did he plant in front?

_____

2. Nelson collected 58 cans of food during his town's food drive. Michael collected 67 cans of food. How many cans of food did they collect altogether?

_____

3. On a snorkeling trip, Betina spotted 27 different kinds of fish. That is 3 times as many as her younger sister Lucia spotted. How many different kinds of fish did Lucia spot?

_____

4. Arnon earned $27 delivering newspapers last week. He spent $9 on a book about snakes. How much money does he have left?

_____

Write a question to finish each word problem. Then solve the problem.

5. Sonya has 272 coins in her collection. Her brother Erez has 298 coins.

Question: _____

_____ Solution: _____

6. Richard folded 32 shirts and stacked them in 4 equal piles.

Question: _____

_____ Solution: _____

Name _____ **Date** _____

Remembering

Write an equation and solve the problem.

1. There are 0 students at the show. The theater had 10 rows of seats. How many students are in each row?

   _____

2. There are 9 vases. Each vase has 3 flowers. How many flowers in all are in the vases?

   _____

Find the unknown number for each Fast Array Drawing.

3.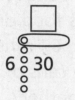

4.

5.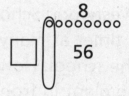

Write an equation to solve the problem.

Show your work.

6. The principal buys 20 new games. He divides them evenly among the 4 third grade classes. How many games does each class receive?

   _____

7. Raj has 4 hooks on his wall. He puts 2 baseball caps on each hook. How many baseball caps does Raj place on the hooks?

   _____

8. **Stretch Your Thinking** Cecelia says she can use addition to solve multiplication problems. Is Cecelia correct? Explain.

   _____

   _____

   _____

Equations and Word Problems

Homework

Write the first step question and answer. Then solve the problem.

1. The tour boats at the Laguna can carry 8 passengers. Jacob watched 6 boats float by. One of the boats had 2 empty seats. The others were full. How many passengers were on the 6 boats?

_____

_____

2. Jerome bought 8 packs of baseball cards at a garage sale. Each pack had 10 cards. He gave his younger sister 3 cards from each pack. How many cards does Jerome have left?

_____

_____

3. Zoe cut a pan of brownies into 4 rows and 6 columns. She divided them evenly among the 8 people at her scout meeting. How many brownies did each person at her scout meeting get?

_____

_____

4. Four girls helped Mr. Day plant a garden. For their help, he gave the girls $24 to share equally. Later, Mrs. Day gave each girl $2 for helping to clean up. How much money did each girl get?

_____

_____

5. Grace made 7 bouquets for the bridesmaids in a wedding. She put 3 roses, 4 tulips, and 2 lilies in each bouquet. How many flowers did she use in all?

_____

_____

Remembering

Write an equation and solve the problem.

1. A toy store owner gives 47 balloons to his customers. He has 7 balloons left. How many balloons did he start with?

_____

2. There are 7 rows of sunflowers in the garden. There are 9 sunflowers in each row. How many sunflowers are in the garden?

Use the pictograph and key to solve.

The basketball team kept track of how many points some players on the team scored in the last game. This pictograph shows how many points some players scored.

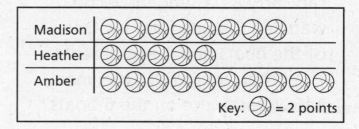

Madison	🏀 🏀 🏀 🏀 🏀 🏀 🏀
Heather	🏀 🏀 🏀 🏀
Amber	🏀 🏀 🏀 🏀 🏀 🏀 🏀 🏀 🏀

Key: 🏀 = 2 points

3. How many points did Amber score?

_____

4. How many more points did Madison score than Heather?

_____

Write an equation and solve the problem.

5. Rita has 90 pages in her notebook. She uses 39 pages. How many pages are left in her notebook?

_____

6. Matt earns $10 for each lawn he mows. How many lawns would he need to mow to earn $80?

_____

7. **Stretch Your Thinking** Write an equation using subtraction and multiplication in which the answer is 36.

_____

Write First Step Questions for Two Step Problems

Homework

> **Study Plan**
>
> Homework Helper

Write an equation and solve the problem.

1. Shamariah collects silk roses. She had 17 silk roses in a vase. Six friends each gave her 3 more roses. How many roses does Shamariah have now?

_____

2. Takala put 9 marbles in the box, Jackie put in 7, and Laird put in 11. Then they divided the marbles evenly among themselves. How many did each person get?

_____

3. A pet store had 9 corn snakes. The snakes laid 8 eggs each. All but 5 of the eggs hatched. How many baby corn snakes does the pet store have?

_____

4. In a paper airplane contest, Amanda's plane flew 19 ft farther than Darren's plane. Darren's plane flew twice as far as Rachel's plane. Rachel's plane flew 20 ft. How far did Amanda's plane fly?

_____

5. Jenna divided 120 daisies into 2 equal groups. Then she divided each group equally into 10 small bunches. She gave her grandmother one small bunch. How many daisies did Jenna give her grandmother?

_____

　　　　　　　Make Sense of Complex Two-Step Word Problems **127**

Name _____ **Date** _____

Remembering

Write an equation and solve the problem.

1. Lily has 24 classmates. She gives each classmate 1 pencil. How many pencils in all does she give her classmates?

2. There are 50 students on a field trip. The tours let 10 students enter at a time. How many tours will be needed for each student to go on a tour?

_____ _____

Write a question to finish the word problem.
Then solve the problem.

3. The art teacher has 9 boxes of crayons. There are 8 crayons in each box.

Question: _____

_____

Solution: _____

Write the first step question and answer. Then solve the problem.

4. Mr. Garcia buys 8 packages of juice. There are 6 juice boxes in each package. On the field trip, 40 students drink a juice box. How many juice boxes are left?

_____

5. Stretch Your Thinking Write a two step word problem that uses multiplication and subtraction. Then solve the two step problem.

_____

_____

_____

_____

_____

Make Sense of Two Step Problems

Homework

Study Plan

_____

Homework Helper

Use a basic multiplication and mental math to complete.

1. 4×4 = _____

4×40 = _____

2. 7×3 = _____

70×3 = _____

3. 6×9 = _____

6×90 = _____

4. 8×7 = _____

8×70 = _____

5. 4×9 = _____

4×90 = _____

6. 2×8 = _____

20×8 = _____

7. 6×5 = _____

60×5 = _____

8. 7×7 = _____

7×70 = _____

9. 5×2 = _____

50×2 = _____

10. 9×80 = _____

11. 30×5 = _____

12. 6×70 = _____

13. 50×4 = _____

14. 90×3 = _____

15. 8×80 = _____

Write an equation and solve the problem.

16. Tom bought 3 packages of cards with 20 cards in each package. How many cards did Tom buy altogether?

_____

17. An orchard has 30 rows of apple trees. There are 3 trees in each row. How many apple trees are in the orchard?

_____

Remembering

Write an equation and solve the problem.

1. The students from Ms. Conner's class are at a show. They are sitting in 4 rows. There are 9 students in each row. How many students from Ms. Conner's class are at the show?

2. Jana's mom bakes 15 muffins for the bake sale. She divides them equally among 3 bags. How many muffins are in each bag?

Write the first step question and answer. Then solve the problem.

3. Gabbie buys 8 packages of plates. There are 8 plates in each package. After the picnic, Gabbie has 4 plates left. How many of Gabbie's plates were used at the picnic?

4. Colin ties 5 groups of balloons to the fence. There are 3 orange balloons, 2 blue balloons, and 4 green balloons in each group. How many balloons does Colin use?

Write an equation and solve the problem.

5. Leanne has 50 red and 22 yellow chenille sticks. She needs 8 chenille sticks for each craft. How many crafts can she make?

6. Mr. Driscoll has 9 reports to grade. There are 6 pages for each report. He grades 12 pages. How many pages does he still have to grade?

7. **Stretch Your Thinking** Write three multiplication equations in which the product will have two zeros. Use 50 as one of the factors.

Name _____   Date _____

Study Plan

_____

Homework Helper

Write an equation and solve the problem.

1. Julia used square tiles to make a design. She laid the tiles in a square, 8 tiles wide by 8 tiles long. Each tile has an area of 1 square inch. What is the area of Julia's tile design?

_____

2. Bart lives 6 blocks from his grandparents. Melinda lives 8 blocks farther from her grandparents as Bart does. How many blocks does Melinda live from her grandparents?

_____

3. Rose rode the roller coaster 9 times. Leila rode the roller coaster 6 less times than Rose. Joseph rode the roller coaster 5 times as many times as Leila. How many times did Joseph ride the roller coaster?

_____

4. Shondra has 40 roses and 40 lilies. She wants to make 8 bouquets with them, with the same number of each type of flower in each bouquet. How many flowers will be in each bouquet?

_____

5. Willis bought a gallon of paint. He painted a wall that is 9 feet high and 10 feet wide. Then he used the rest of the paint to paint 46 square feet in the hall. How many square feet did the gallon of paint cover?

_____

6. Randall bought 7 computer games at a yard sale. He paid $4 each for 6 of the games, and $5 for the other game. How much money did he spend?

_____

Name _____ Date _____

Remembering

Write an equation and solve the problem.

1. There are 40 students at the picnic. There are 5 picnic tables. The same number of students is at each table. How many students are at each table?

_____

2. Claire puts $2 in her coin purse each day for 7 days. How much money is in her coin purse after 7 days?

_____

Write an equation and solve the problem.

3. There are 4 rows of carrots in the garden. Six carrots are in each row. The farmer picks 3 of the carrots. How many carrots are still in the garden?

_____

4. Darla uses 3 pink roses and 4 yellow tulips to fill each vase. She fills 7 vases. How many flowers does she use?

_____

Use a basic multiplication and mental math to complete.

5. $6 \times 3 =$ _____

   $60 \times 3 =$ _____

6. $7 \times 9 =$ _____

   $7 \times 90 =$ _____

7. $4 \times 2 =$ _____

   $40 \times 2 =$ _____

8. $8 \times 4 =$ _____

   $80 \times 4 =$ _____

9. $2 \times 5 =$ _____

   $2 \times 50 =$ _____

10. $3 \times 4 =$ _____

   $30 \times 4 =$ _____

11. $5 \times 80 =$ _____

12. $90 \times 8 =$ _____

13. $6 \times 70 =$ _____

14. **Stretch Your Thinking** I am a multiple of 10. My factors include an even number and an odd number. I am greater than 3×5 and less than 4×7. What number am I?

_____

Play Multiplication and Division Games

2×2	$2 \cdot 3$	$2 * 4$	2×5
	Hint: What is $3 \cdot 2$?	Hint: What is $4 * 2$?	Hint: What is 5×2?

2×6	$2 \cdot 7$	$2 * 8$	2×9
Hint: What is 6×2?	Hint: What is $7 \cdot 2$?	Hint: What is $8 * 2$?	Hint: What is 9×2?

5×2	$5 \cdot 3$	$5 * 4$	5×5
Hint: What is 2×5?	Hint: What is $3 \cdot 5$?	Hint: What is $4 * 5$?	

5×6	$5 \cdot 7$	$5 * 8$	5×9
Hint: What is 6×5?	Hint: What is $7 \cdot 5$?	Hint: What is $8 * 5$?	Hint: What is 9×5?

$2\overline{)10}$

Hint: What is
☐ × 2 = 10?

$2\overline{)8}$

Hint: What is
☐ × 2 = 8?

$2\overline{)6}$

Hint: What is
☐ × 2 = 6?

$2\overline{)4}$

Hint: What is
☐ × 2 = 4?

$2\overline{)18}$

Hint: What is
☐ × 2 = 18?

$2\overline{)16}$

Hint: What is
☐ × 2 = 16?

$2\overline{)14}$

Hint: What is
☐ × 2 = 14?

$2\overline{)12}$

Hint: What is
☐ × 2 = 12?

$5\overline{)25}$

Hint: What is
☐ × 5 = 25?

$5\overline{)20}$

Hint: What is
☐ × 5 = 20?

$5\overline{)15}$

Hint: What is
☐ × 5 = 15?

$5\overline{)10}$

Hint: What is
☐ × 5 = 10?

$5\overline{)45}$

Hint: What is
☐ × 5 = 45?

$5\overline{)40}$

Hint: What is
☐ × 5 = 40?

$5\overline{)35}$

Hint: What is
☐ × 5 = 35?

$5\overline{)30}$

Hint: What is
☐ × 5 = 30?

Home Product Cards: 2s, 5s, 9s

9×2	$9 \cdot 3$	$9 * 4$	9×5

Hint:
What is 2×9?
© Houghton Mifflin Harcourt Publishing Company

Hint:
What is $3 \cdot 9$?
© Houghton Mifflin Harcourt Publishing Company

Hint:
What is $4 * 9$?
© Houghton Mifflin Harcourt Publishing Company

Hint:
What is 5×9?
© Houghton Mifflin Harcourt Publishing Company

9×6	$9 \cdot 7$	$9 * 8$	9×9

Hint:
What is 6×9?
© Houghton Mifflin Harcourt Publishing Company

Hint:
What is $7 \cdot 9$?
© Houghton Mifflin Harcourt Publishing Company

Hint:
What is $8 * 9$?
© Houghton Mifflin Harcourt Publishing Company

© Houghton Mifflin Harcourt Publishing Company

$\times$ $\bullet$ $*$ $\times$

$\times$ $\bullet$ $*$ $\times$

You can write any numbers on the last 8 cards. Use them to practice difficult problems or if you lose a card.

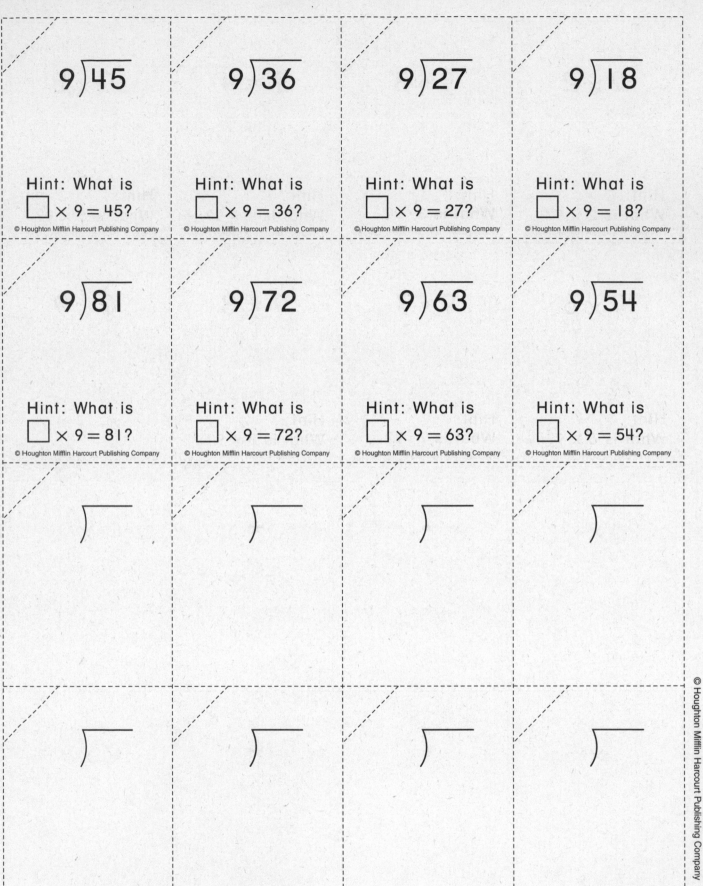

$9)\overline{45}$

Hint: What is $\square \times 9 = 45$?

$9)\overline{36}$

Hint: What is $\square \times 9 = 36$?

$9)\overline{27}$

Hint: What is $\square \times 9 = 27$?

$9)\overline{18}$

Hint: What is $\square \times 9 = 18$?

$9)\overline{81}$

Hint: What is $\square \times 9 = 81$?

$9)\overline{72}$

Hint: What is $\square \times 9 = 72$?

$9)\overline{63}$

Hint: What is $\square \times 9 = 63$?

$9)\overline{54}$

Hint: What is $\square \times 9 = 54$?

You can write any numbers on the last 8 cards. Use them to practice difficult problems or if you lose a card.

Home Product Cards: 2s, 5s, 9s

3×2	$3 \cdot 3$	$3 * 4$	3×5
Hint: What is 2×3? © Houghton Mifflin Harcourt Publishing Company	© Houghton Mifflin Harcourt Publishing Company	Hint: What is $4 * 3$? © Houghton Mifflin Harcourt Publishing Company	Hint: What is 5×3? © Houghton Mifflin Harcourt Publishing Company
3×6	$3 \cdot 7$	$3 * 8$	3×9
Hint: What is 6×3? © Houghton Mifflin Harcourt Publishing Company	Hint: What is $7 \cdot 3$? © Houghton Mifflin Harcourt Publishing Company	Hint: What is $8 * 3$? © Houghton Mifflin Harcourt Publishing Company	Hint: What is 9×3? © Houghton Mifflin Harcourt Publishing Company
4×2	$4 \cdot 3$	$4 * 4$	4×5
Hint: What is 2×4? © Houghton Mifflin Harcourt Publishing Company	Hint: What is $3 \cdot 4$? © Houghton Mifflin Harcourt Publishing Company	© Houghton Mifflin Harcourt Publishing Company	Hint: What is 5×4? © Houghton Mifflin Harcourt Publishing Company
4×6	$4 \cdot 7$	$4 * 8$	4×9
Hint: What is 6×4? © Houghton Mifflin Harcourt Publishing Company	Hint: What is $7 \cdot 4$? © Houghton Mifflin Harcourt Publishing Company	Hint: What is $8 * 4$? © Houghton Mifflin Harcourt Publishing Company	Hint: What is 9×4? © Houghton Mifflin Harcourt Publishing Company

$3\overline{)15}$

Hint: What is

$\square \times 3 = 15?$

$3\overline{)12}$

Hint: What is

$\square \times 3 = 12?$

$3\overline{)9}$

Hint: What is

$\square \times 3 = 9?$

$3\overline{)6}$

Hint: What is

$\square \times 3 = 6?$

$3\overline{)27}$

Hint: What is

$\square \times 3 = 27?$

$3\overline{)24}$

Hint: What is

$\square \times 3 = 24?$

$3\overline{)21}$

Hint: What is

$\square \times 3 = 21?$

$3\overline{)18}$

Hint: What is

$\square \times 3 = 18?$

$4\overline{)20}$

Hint: What is

$\square \times 4 = 20?$

$4\overline{)16}$

Hint: What is

$\square \times 4 = 16?$

$4\overline{)12}$

Hint: What is

$\square \times 4 = 12?$

$4\overline{)8}$

Hint: What is

$\square \times 4 = 8?$

$4\overline{)36}$

Hint: What is

$\square \times 4 = 36?$

$4\overline{)32}$

Hint: What is

$\square \times 4 = 32?$

$4\overline{)28}$

Hint: What is

$\square \times 4 = 28?$

$4\overline{)24}$

Hint: What is

$\square \times 4 = 24?$

Home Product Cards: 3s, 4s

6×2	$6 \cdot 3$	$6 * 4$	6×5

Hint:
What is 2×6?

Hint:
What is $3 \cdot 6$?

Hint:
What is $4 * 6$?

Hint:
What is 5×6?

$$6 \times 6 \qquad 6 \cdot 7 \qquad 6 * 8 \qquad 6 \times 9$$

Hint:
What is $7 \cdot 6$?

Hint:
What is $8 * 6$?

Hint:
What is 9×6?

$$7 \times 2 \qquad 7 \cdot 3 \qquad 7 * 4 \qquad 7 \times 5$$

Hint:
What is 2×7?

Hint:
What is $3 \cdot 7$?

Hint:
What is $4 * 7$?

Hint:
What is 5×7?

$$7 \times 6 \qquad 7 \cdot 7 \qquad 7 * 8 \qquad 7 \times 9$$

Hint:
What is 6×7?

Hint:
What is $8 * 7$?

Hint:
What is 9×7?

$6 \overline{)30}$

Hint: What is
$\square \times 6 = 30?$

$6 \overline{)24}$

Hint: What is
$\square \times 6 = 24?$

$6 \overline{)18}$

Hint: What is
$\square \times 6 = 18?$

$6 \overline{)12}$

Hint: What is
$\square \times 6 = 12?$

$6 \overline{)54}$

Hint: What is
$\square \times 6 = 54?$

$6 \overline{)48}$

Hint: What is
$\square \times 6 = 48?$

$6 \overline{)42}$

Hint: What is
$\square \times 6 = 42?$

$6 \overline{)36}$

Hint: What is
$\square \times 6 = 36?$

$7 \overline{)35}$

Hint: What is
$\square \times 7 = 35?$

$7 \overline{)28}$

Hint: What is
$\square \times 7 = 28?$

$7 \overline{)21}$

Hint: What is
$\square \times 7 = 21?$

$7 \overline{)14}$

Hint: What is
$\square \times 7 = 14?$

$7 \overline{)63}$

Hint: What is
$\square \times 7 = 63?$

$7 \overline{)56}$

Hint: What is
$\square \times 7 = 56?$

$7 \overline{)49}$

Hint: What is
$\square \times 7 = 49?$

$7 \overline{)42}$

Hint: What is
$\square \times 7 = 42?$

Home Product Cards: 2s, 5s, 9s

8×2

Hint:
What is 2×8?
© Houghton Mifflin Harcourt Publishing Company

$8 \cdot 3$

Hint:
What is $3 \cdot 8$?
© Houghton Mifflin Harcourt Publishing Company

$8 * 4$

Hint:
What is $4 * 8$?
© Houghton Mifflin Harcourt Publishing Company

8×5

Hint:
What is 5×8?
© Houghton Mifflin Harcourt Publishing Company

8×6

Hint:
What is 6×8?
© Houghton Mifflin Harcourt Publishing Company

$8 \cdot 7$

Hint:
What is $7 \cdot 8$?
© Houghton Mifflin Harcourt Publishing Company

$8 * 8$

8×9

Hint:
What is 9×8?
© Houghton Mifflin Harcourt Publishing Company

$\times$

$\cdot$

$*$

$\times$

$\times$

$\cdot$

$*$

$\times$

You can write any numbers on the last 8 cards. Use them to practice difficult problems or if you lose a card.

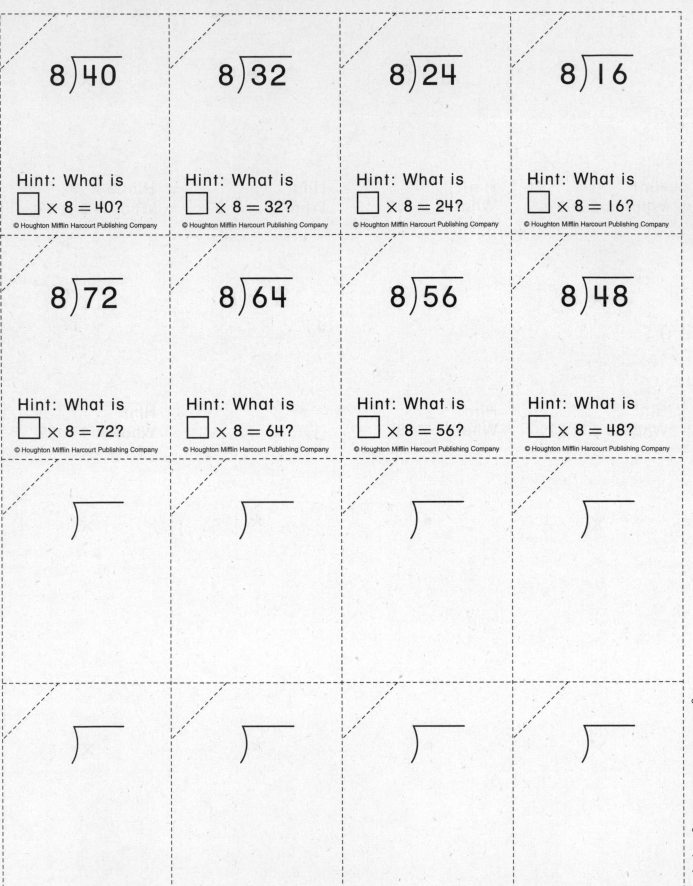

$8\overline{)40}$

Hint: What is
$\square \times 8 = 40$?

$8\overline{)32}$

Hint: What is
$\square \times 8 = 32$?

$8\overline{)24}$

Hint: What is
$\square \times 8 = 24$?

$8\overline{)16}$

Hint: What is
$\square \times 8 = 16$?

$8\overline{)72}$

Hint: What is
$\square \times 8 = 72$?

$8\overline{)64}$

Hint: What is
$\square \times 8 = 64$?

$8\overline{)56}$

Hint: What is
$\square \times 8 = 56$?

$8\overline{)48}$

Hint: What is
$\square \times 8 = 48$?

You can write any numbers on the last 8 cards. Use them to practice difficult problems or if you lose a card.

Home Product Cards: 6s, 7s, 8s

Homework

Study Plan

_____

Homework Helper

Complete.

1. $6 \times 3 =$ _____

2. $7 \times 9 =$ _____

3. $4 \times 0 =$ _____

4. $30 \div 5 =$ _____

5. $18 \div 2 =$ _____

6. $70 \div 7 =$ _____

7. $36 \div$ _____ $= 9$

8. $3 \times$ _____ $= 24$

9. _____ $\div 8 = 0$

10. _____ $\times 7 = 35$

11. $60 =$ _____ $\times 6$

12. $4 = 28 \div$ _____

13. $72 = 8 \times$ _____

14. $2 =$ _____ $\div 10$

15. _____ $= 45 \div 9$

16. $21 =$ _____ $\times 7$

17. $8 = 64 \div$ _____

18. _____ $\times 374 = 0$

Solve.

19. Using only whole numbers, Nikki wrote as many multiplication equations as she could with 12 as the product. What were her equations?

_____

_____

20. Pablo wrote four division equations with 6 as the quotient. What could have been the four division equations that he wrote?

_____

_____

Remembering

Write an equation and solve the problem.

1. Stephen has a stamp collection of 72 stamps. He puts 9 stamps on each page in his album. How many pages does he fill?

_____

2. There are 6 birdcages at the zoo. Two birds are in each birdcage. How many birds are in the birdcages?

_____

Use a basic multiplication and mental math to complete.

3. $2 \times 8 =$ _____

   $20 \times 8 =$ _____

4. $5 \times 9 =$ _____

   $5 \times 90 =$ _____

5. $3 \times 7 =$ _____

   $30 \times 7 =$ _____

6. $6 \times 4 =$ _____

   $60 \times 4 =$ _____

7. $9 \times 4 =$ _____

   $9 \times 40 =$ _____

8. $5 \times 5 =$ _____

   $50 \times 5 =$ _____

9. $7 \times 80 =$ _____

10. $70 \times 7 =$ _____

11. $6 \times 60 =$ _____

Write an equation and solve the problem.

12. Max has $12 for the field trip. Sue has $4 less than Max. Ellen has $2 more than Sue. How much money does Ellen have for the field trip?

_____

13. Jeremiah mows 8 lawns. Andy mows 4 fewer lawns than Jeremiah. Sally mows double the number Andy mows. How many lawns does Sally mow?

_____

14. **Stretch Your Thinking** Write three multiplication equations in which the product is 24. Then draw an array for one of your equations.

_____

Homework

A zoo kitchen's weekly grocery list shows the zoo orders 56 pounds of bananas each week. The zoo kitchen uses the same number of pounds of bananas each day.

1. Complete the chart showing the number of pounds of bananas the zoo kitchen has used after each day of the week.

Number of Days	1	2	3	4	5	6	7
Number of Pounds of Bananas							56

2. Write an equation to show how to find the number of pounds of bananas the zoo uses in one day.

_____

Write an equation and solve the problem.

3. The zoo uses 10 pounds of apples each day. How many pounds of apples should be on the weekly grocery list?

_____

4. After 6 days, how many pounds of apples does the zoo use?

_____

5. After 6 days, how many more pounds of apples than bananas does the zoo use?

_____

6. How many pounds of bananas and apples altogether does the zoo use each week?

_____

© Houghton Mifflin Harcourt Publishing Company

Remembering

Write an equation and solve the problem.

1. Tami uses square tiles to make an array. She places 5 tiles in each row. She makes 5 rows. How many square tiles does she use?

_____

2. Mrs. Gibbs sets up 36 chairs for parents to watch the class performance. She makes 4 rows. How many chairs are in each row?

_____

Write an equation and solve the problem.

3. There are 163 adults and 37 students in the audience. Will 4 packages of 50 programs be enough for each person in the audience to receive a program? Explain.

_____

4. There were 8 rows of picture frames at the store. There are 7 picture frames in each row. Twelve picture frames are sold. How many picture frames are left at the store?

_____

Complete.

5. $40 \div 10 =$ _____

6. _____ $= 8 \times 3$

7. _____ $\times 4 = 28$

8. $2 \times 4 =$ _____

9. _____ $= 8 \times 8$

10. _____ $= 81 \div 9$

11. $9 \times 5 =$ _____

12. $42 \div$ _____ $= 6$

13. $9 \times$ _____ $= 63$

14. **Stretch Your Thinking** Matt runs four days a week. On the first day he runs 30 minutes. On the second day he runs 5 minutes more than on the first day. On the third day he runs the same number of minutes as the second day. On the fourth day he runs 10 minutes more than the previous day. After Matt runs on the fourth day, how many minutes in all has he run?

_____

Homework

Estimate the length of the line segment in inches.
Then measure it to the nearest inch.

1. ▬▬▬▬▬▬▬▬▬▬▬▬▬▬

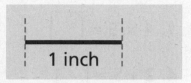

| ⊢———⊣ |
| 1 inch |

Estimate: _____ Actual: _____

Estimate the length of the line segment in inches. Then measure it to the nearest $\frac{1}{2}$ inch.

2. ▬▬▬▬▬▬▬▬▬▬

Estimate: _____ Actual: _____

Estimate the length of each line segment in inches.
Then measure it to the nearest $\frac{1}{4}$ inch.

3. ▬▬▬▬▬

Estimate: _____ Actual: _____

4. ▬▬▬▬▬▬▬▬▬▬▬▬▬

Estimate: _____ Actual: _____

Draw a line segment that has the given length.

5. 4 inches

6. $3\frac{1}{4}$ inches

7. $4\frac{1}{2}$ inches

8. $\frac{3}{4}$ inch

9. Marta wants to make 4 necklaces that are the same length. She asks her friends to cut the string for the necklaces 15 paper clips long. Would all the lengths be the same? Explain your thinking.

_____

_____

Remembering

Solve each equation.

1. $4 \times 5 = \boxed{}$
　　　　　　2. $10 * 5 = \boxed{}$
　　　　　　3. $3 \cdot 5 = \boxed{}$

4. $2 * 5 = \boxed{}$
　　　　　　5. $1 \cdot 5 = \boxed{}$
　　　　　　6. $5 \times 9 = \boxed{}$

7. $5 \cdot 7 = \boxed{}$
　　　　　　8. $5 * 5 = \boxed{}$
　　　　　　9. $5 \times 6 = \boxed{}$

Solve each problem.

10. Tommy buys 6 notebooks. They cost $3 each. How much does he spend?

_____

11. Olivia has 42 muffins. She puts the same number of muffins into each of 6 baskets. How many muffins does Olivia put in each basket?

_____

Solve each problem. Label your answers with the correct units.

12. Ms. Emerson has a rectangular shelf that is 5 feet long and 3 feet wide. What is the area of the shelf?

_____

13. Trevor has a rectangular treasure box with an area of 72 square centimeters. If the length of one side is 9 centimeters, what is the length of the adjacent side?

_____

14. Stretch Your Thinking Grace has a piece of string that is 8 inches long. She needs to cut the string into four equal pieces, but she does not have a ruler. Explain a way Grace can cut the string into four equal pieces.

_____

_____

Homework

Choose the best unit to measure how much each item can hold. Write *cup*, *pint*, *quart*, or *gallon*.

1. a bathtub _____

2. a container of orange juice _____

3. a juice box _____

4. a small milk carton _____

Use drawings to represent the problems.

5. Molly bought a container of lemonade that had 6 cups. She drank 2 cups. How many cups of lemonade does she have left?

_____

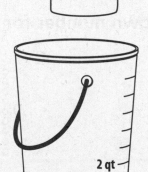

1 cup

6. Randy poured 8 quarts of water in a bucket. Then he added 4 more quarts. How many quarts of water are in the bucket?

_____

2 qt

Solve. Use drawings if you need to.

7. Mrs. Sanders buys 2 gallons of milk each week. How many gallons of milk will she buy in 10 weeks?

_____

8. Brianna bought 64 fluid ounces of her favorite drink. How many 8 fluid-ounce glasses can she fill with the drink?

_____

9. Brian's aquarium holds 16 gallons of water. He uses 2-gallon containers of water to fill the aquarium. How many containers does he use?

10. The Corner Market sold 24 pints of milk on Monday and 18 pints on Tuesday. How many pints of milk did the market sell on those two days?

Remembering

Make a math drawing for the problem and label it with a multiplication equation. Then write the answer.

1. Coach Stevens puts 6 cones in each row for physical education class. He makes 4 rows. How many cones does Coach Stevens use?

   _____

2. Emily puts stickers in 8 bags, with 5 stickers per bag. How many stickers does Emily use?

   _____

Find the unknown number for each Fast Array drawing.

3.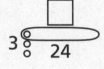
    3   24

4. 6

    9

5. 4
    20

Estimate the length of the line segment in inches. Then measure it to the nearest $\frac{1}{2}$ inch.

6. ▬▬▬▬▬▬▬▬▬▬▬▬   ▬▬▬▬
                                   1 inch

   Estimate: _____ Actual: _____

8. **Stretch Your Thinking** Write a word problem in which the answer is 6 gallons.

   _____

   _____

Name _____ Date _____

1 liter (L) = 1,000 milliliters (mL)

Circle the better estimate.

1. a container of milk 2 L 20 mL

2. a cup of punch 25 L 250 mL

3. an eyedropper 1 L or 1 mL

4. a jar of pickles 50 L 500 mL

Choose the unit you would use to measure the liquid volume of each. Write *mL* or *L*.

5. a container of glue _____

6. an aquarium _____

Use the drawing to represent and solve the problem.

7. Dinah had a bottle of water that contained 800 milliliters of water. She used 500 milliliters. How much water is left in the bottle?

_____

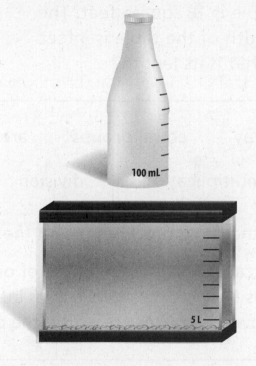

8. Galen has a fish tank that holds 40 liters of water. He poured 15 liters of water into the tank. How many more liters does he need to add to fill the tank?

_____

Solve.

9. Ben has 4 hummingbird feeders. Each feeder holds 80 milliliters of liquid hummingbird food. How many milliliters of liquid hummingbird food does Ben need?

_____

10. Drew needs 27 liters of punch for a party. It comes in 3 liter containers. How many containers should Drew buy?

_____

Name _____ **Date** _____

Remembering

Make a math drawing for the problem and label it with a multiplication equation. Then write the answer to the problem.

1. Kelly's garden has 6 rows of tulips. There are 5 tulips in each row. How many tulips are in her garden?

   _____

Solve. Then circle what type it is and what operation you used.

2. The area of the rectangular table is 18 square feet. The width of the table is 3 feet. What is its length?

   _____

   array   equal groups   area

   multiplication   division

3. The band lines up in 8 rows, with 6 band members in each row. How many band members are there in all?

   _____

   array   equal groups   area

   multiplication   division

Use the drawing to represent the problem.

4. Elizabeth buys a container of orange juice that has 8 cups. She pours 6 cups into a pitcher. How many cups are left in the container?

   _____

1 cup

5. **Stretch Your Thinking** Write a word problem that involves subtracting 4 liters. Then solve. Draw a picture to represent your answer.

   _____

   _____

   _____

Metric Units of Liquid Volume

Homework

Choose the unit you would use to measure the weight of each object. Write _ounce_ or _pound_.

1.

_____

2.

_____

3.

_____

Choose the unit you would use to measure the mass of each object. Write _gram_ or _kilogram_.

4.

_____

5.

_____

6.

_____

Circle the better estimate.

7. a pillow   8 oz   8 lb   8. a stapler   250 g   250 kg

9. a car   1,000 g   1,000 kg   10. a large book   3 lb   30 lb

Solve. Use a drawing if you need to.

11. Steve bought 24 ounces of his favorite cereal. He put equal amounts of the cereal in 4 containers. How many ounces did he put in each container?

_____

12. Beth bought a bag filled with 340 grams of pasta. She used 250 grams. How many grams are left in the bag?

_____

13. There are 8 books in a box. Each book has a mass of 2 kilograms. What is the total mass of the books?

_____

14. Roy bought a 25-pound bag and a 10-pound bag of pet food. How many pounds of pet food did he buy?

_____

Remembering

Write an equation and solve the problem.

1. The shoe store has a stack of 9 shoeboxes. Two shoes are in each box. How many shoes are in the stack?

   _____

2. Mrs. Rak's class has 35 students. Seven students sit at each table. How many tables of students are there?

   _____

Multiply or divide to find the unknown numbers.

3. $50 \div 10 = \boxed{}$

4. $2 * \boxed{} = 14$

5. $6\overline{)54} = \boxed{}$

6. $6 \cdot 4 = \boxed{}$

7. $\frac{49}{7} = \boxed{}$

8. $\boxed{} \times 4 = 20$

Use drawings to represent the problems.

9. Meagan has a container that has 700 milliliters of milk. She uses 300 milliliters for a recipe. How much milk is left in the container?

   _____

100 mL

10. Austin puts 5 liters of water in an empty bucket. Miles puts in another 8 liters. How much water is in the bucket now?

    _____

1 L

11. **Stretch Your Thinking** Explain how you know whether to choose grams or kilograms when measuring mass. Name an object you would measure using each unit.

    _____

Customary Units of Weight and Metric Units of Mass

Homework

Name _____ Date _____

Solve. Use drawings if you need to.   *Show Your Work*

1. Carlie had 800 milliliters of water in a container.
   She poured all but 300 milliliters into a vase.
   How many milliliters of water did Carlie pour
   into the vase?

   _____

2. Benji bought 2 potatoes that together have a mass
   of 496 grams. If one potato has a mass of 254 grams,
   what is the mass of the other potato?

   _____

3. An average sized duck egg has a mass of 80 grams.
   What would be the mass of three duck eggs?

   _____

4. Michelle has 4 buckets she uses to water plants.
   She filled each bucket with 6 liters of water.
   What is the total liquid volume of all the buckets?

   _____

5. A stack of books has a mass of 21 kilograms. If each
   book in the stack has a mass of 3 kilograms, how
   many books are in the stack?

   _____

6. Martha bought a liter of lemonade. She gave each
   of her 3 friends 300 milliliters. Did Martha use the
   whole liter of lemonade? Explain.

   _____

   _____

Remembering

Multiply or divide to find the unknown numbers.

1. $\dfrac{40}{8}$ = ☐

2. $5 * $ ☐ $= 50$

3. $2\overline{)10}$ = ☐

4. $6 \cdot 10 = $ ☐

5. $90 \div 10 = $ ☐

6. ☐ $\times 4 = 20$

Solve.

7. The valet parked 5 rows of cars in the parking lot.
   He put 5 cars in each row. How many cars
   did he park?

   _____

8. Charlie is making a mosaic picture using
   1-centimeter square tiles. He places them in a
   square, 8 tiles wide by 8 tiles long. What is the
   area of the mosaic picture?

   _____

**Choose the unit you would use to measure the
weight of each object. Write *ounce* or *pound*.**

9.

10.

11.

_____ _____ _____

12. **Stretch Your Thinking** Jake has 12 liters of water.
    Name four different ways he can divide the water into
    buckets so each bucket has the same number of liters.

    _____

    _____

Solve Word Problems

Homework

Write the time on the digital clock. Then write how to say the time.

1.

_____

2.

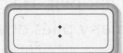

_____

3.

_____

4.

_____

Draw the hands on the anolog clock. Write the time on the digital clock.

5. twenty-eight minutes after four

6. six forty-five

7. quarter to seven

Write the time on the digital clock. Then write how to say the time.

8.

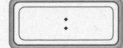

_____

9.

_____

10.

_____

Remembering

Write an equation and solve the problem.

1. The pet store has 7 aquariums. There are 9 fish in each aquarium. How many fish in all are in the aquariums?

   _____

2. Declan has 81 dollar bills. He puts them in piles of 9. How many piles does he make?

   _____

Find the unknown number for each Fast Array drawing.

3.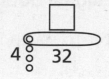

4.

5.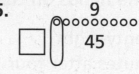

Solve.

6. LaDonna buys 2 grapefruits that together have a mass of 479 grams. If one grapefruit has a mass of 245 grams, what is the mass of the other grapefruit?

   _____

7. Harper fills 3 pots each with 4 liters of water. How many liters of water does he pour into the pots?

   _____

8. **Stretch Your Thinking** I am an hour that happens two times a day. My hands point in opposite directions. Both my hands point to a number on the clock. What hour am I?

   _____

Name _____ **Date** _____

Homework

Write the times as minutes *after* an hour and minutes *before* an hour.

1.

_____

_____

2.

_____

_____

3.

_____

_____

4.

_____

_____

5.

_____

_____

6.

_____

_____

7.

_____

_____

8.

_____

_____

9.

_____

_____

Remembering

Multiply or divide to find the unknown numbers.

1. $\frac{36}{9} = \boxed{}$

2. $40 \div 5 = \boxed{}$

3. $2 \cdot 7 = \boxed{}$

4. $7 \times 5 = \boxed{}$

5. $10\overline{)90} = \boxed{}$

6. $10 * 8 = \boxed{}$

Write an equation to solve the problem.

7. Antonio is planting bean seeds. He puts 6 seeds in each row. There are 5 rows. How many bean seeds does he plant?

_____

8. The baker made 56 fresh baked muffins. There are 8 muffins in each tin. How many tins did he use?

_____

Write the time on the digital clock. Then write how to say the time.

9.
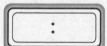

10.

11.

12.
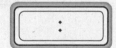

_____ _____ _____ _____

13. **Stretch Your Thinking** List five different times in which the minutes before are the same as the minutes after the hour.

_____

Before and After the Hour

Complete.

1. Complete the table.

Start Time	Elapsed Time	End Time
2:00 P.M.		10:00 P.M.
2:27 A.M.		4:45 A.M.
3:30 A.M.	1 hour and 22 minutes	
2:10 P.M.	3 hours and 16 minutes	
	2 hours and ten minutes	11:00 A.M.
	4 hours and 39 minutes	7:53 P.M.

Solve. Use your clock if you need to.

2. Liza left the library at 11:30 A.M. on Saturday.
She had been there for 1 hour and 25 minutes.
What time did she get to the library?

_____

3. Andres spent from 4:15 P.M. to 5:05 P.M. doing
chores. How much time did Andres spend
doing his chores?

_____

4. Arjun arrived at baseball practice at 5:15 P.M.
He practiced for 1 hour and 30 minutes.
What time did baseball practice end?

_____

5. Today Sarah's piano lessons started at 4:15 P.M.
She was finished with her lessons at 5:10 P.M.
How long was Sarah at piano lessons?

_____

Remembering

Multiply or divide to find the unknown numbers.

1. $\frac{30}{3}$ = ☐

2. 27 ÷ 9 = ☐

3. 2 • 3 = ☐

4. 7 × 9 = ☐

5. 5)‾20 = ☐

6. 4 * 3 = ☐

Write an equation and solve the problem.

7. There are 36 students at the show. They sit in 4 equal rows. How many seats are in each row?

_____

8. The music teacher set up 67 chairs for the concert. The principal set up 35 chairs for the concert. How many chairs in all did they set up?

_____

Write the times as minutes *after* an hour and minutes *before* an hour.

9.

10.

11.

_____   _____   _____

_____   _____   _____

12. **Stretch Your Thinking** Write a word problem where something starts at 8:25 A.M. and ends at 1:43 P.M.

_____

_____

_____

_____

Elapsed Time

Homework

Solve using a number line.

1. Terry began watching a movie at 5:45 P.M. The movie lasted 2 hours 20 minutes. Then Terry spent 25 minutes eating a snack. What time did Terry finish eating the snack?

5:30   6:00   6:30   7:00   7:30   8:00   8:30

_____

2. Evan left his friend's house at 5:00 P.M. He had been there 2 hours 15 minutes. At what time did Evan arrive at his friend's house?

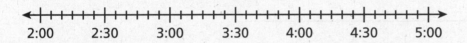

2:00   2:30   3:00   3:30   4:00   4:30   5:00

_____

3. Haley began reading her book at 9:55 A.M. She read for 1 hour 35 minutes. Then she spent 45 minutes doing homework. What time did Haley finish her homework?

9:00   9:30   ↑10:00   10:30   11:00   11:30   12:00   12:30
                9:55 A.M.

_____

4. Myra left home at 12:45 P.M. She spent 30 minutes eating lunch and 50 minutes watching a parade. Then it took her 15 minutes to drive home. What time did Myra return home?

12:00   12:30   1:00   1:30   2:00   2:30   3:00

_____

Name _____   **Date** _____

Remembering

Make a rectangle drawing to represent each exercise.
Then find the product.

1. 6 × 9 = _____   **2.** 7 * 5 = _____   **3.** 3 • 6 = _____

Write the first step question and answer.
Then solve the problem.

4. The baker makes 54 biscuits in the morning.
Then he makes 26 more in the afternoon.
He puts 10 biscuits in each bag. How many
bags does he fill?

_____

_____

5. Complete the table.

Start Time	Elapsed Time	End Time
9:32 A.M.	1 hour 23 minutes	
1:19 P.M.		5:37 P.M.
	2 hours 45 minutes	7:31 P.M.

6. Stretch Your Thinking Write a two step time
word problem using the number line in which
the start time is 4:50. Use the number line below
to show how to solve.

4:00   4:30   5:00   5:30   6:00   6:30   7:00

_____

_____

_____

Add and Subtract Time

Homework

Solve. Use a clock or sketch a number line diagram if you need to.

1. Rhea arrived at the mall at 3:45 P.M. She spent 45 minutes having lunch and then she shopped for 55 minutes before leaving the mall. How much time did Rhea spend at the mall?

_____

2. Mrs. Cox is baking a ham for dinner. It takes 1 hour 30 minutes to bake. The family eats at 6:15 P.M. What time should Mrs. Cox put the ham in the oven?

_____

3. Dina started chores at 8:15 A.M. and finished at 9:05 A.M. It took her 30 minutes to clean her room and she spent the rest of the time bathing her dog. How long did Dina spend bathing her dog?

_____

4. Jerry finished skating at 7:00 P.M. He skated for 1 hour 45 minutes. What time did he start skating?

_____

5. Jason started his project at 2:30 P.M. and finished 2 hours and 15 minutes later. He spent 25 minutes doing research, 30 minutes writing a report, and the rest of the time building a model. What time did he finish his project? How much time did he spend building the model?

_____

Solve Word Problems Involving Time **165**

Remembering

Solve each problem.   *Show Your Work*

1. The farmer makes stacks of 4 bales of hay. He makes 6 stacks. How many bales of hay does he stack?

_____

2. Lilly has 85 shells in her collection. She gives 13 shells to her best friend. She puts the rest of her shells in groups of 9. How many groups does she make?

_____

Solve.

3. William and Hannah went to the bowling alley at 5:30 P.M. They bowled for 1 hour 20 minutes. Then they played a video game for 30 minutes. After the video game, they leave to go home. What time did they leave?

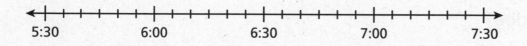

5:30   6:00   6:30   7:00   7:30

_____

_____

4. **Stretch Your Thinking** Tony is cooking dinner. He starts cooking at different times, so all the foods will be ready at the same time. The chicken takes 25 minutes to cook, the rice takes 40 minutes to cook, and the green beans take 15 minutes to cook. All the foods are finished at 5:33 P.M. At what time did he start cooking each food?

_____

_____

     Solve Word Problems

3-11

Homework

Name   **Date**

Use the horizontal bar graph to answer each question.

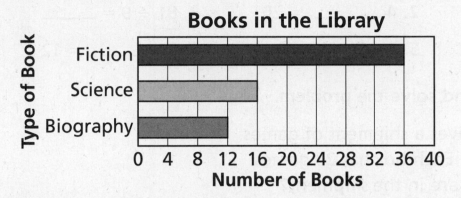

1. How many fiction books are in the library? _____

2. How many more science books are there than biographies? _____

3. Write two of your own questions that can be answered using the graph.

Use the vertical bar graph to answer each question.

4. How many cats and dogs are at the kennel? _____

5. The kennel has the fewest of which type of pet? _____

6. Write two of your own questions that can be answered using the graph.

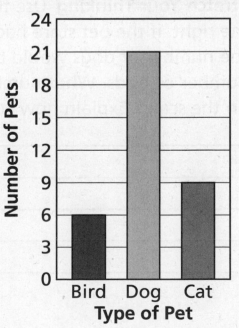

© Houghton Mifflin Harcourt Publishing Company

UNIT 3 LESSON 11   Read and Create Pictographs and Bar Graphs **167**

Remembering

Multiply or divide.

1. $7 * 3 =$ _____

2. $4 \times$ _____ $= 20$

3. $81 \div 9 =$ _____

4. $\dfrac{8}{2} =$ _____

5. $5 \cdot 9 =$ _____

6. $2 \times$ _____ $= 12$

Write an equation and solve the problem.

7. The toy store receives a shipment of games. There are 8 boxes. Each box has 20 games. How many games are in the shipment?

_____

Solve. Use a clock or sketch a number line diagram to help you.

8. Emily arrives at school at 8:35 A.M. Together reading and math last for 1 hour 35 minutes. Then Emily goes to band practice for 45 minutes. What time does band practice end?

_____

9. Stretch Your Thinking Use the graph at the right. If the pet store had 10 more birds, the number of dogs would be double the number of birds. What numbers should be on the scale? Explain how you solved.

_____

_____

_____

_____

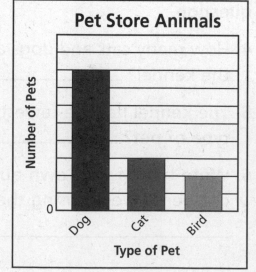

Pet Store Animals

Homework

Use the vertical bar graph to answer the questions.

Sunnytown Reading Festival

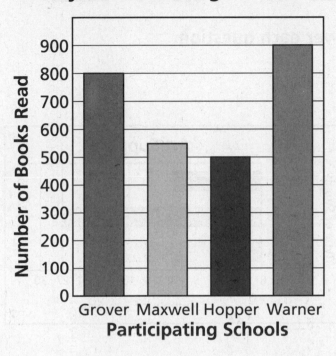

Number of Books Read

900
800
700
600
500
400
300
200
100
0

Grover Maxwell Hopper Warner
Participating Schools

1. About how many books did students at Maxwell School read?

_____

2. How many more books did students at Grover School read than students at Hopper School?

_____

3. How many fewer books did students at Hopper School read than students at Warner School?

_____

4. How many more books did the students at Maxwell need to read to have the same number of books as Warner?

_____

5. Use the information in this table to make a vertical bar graph.

Pinball Scores

Player	Points
Trina	500
Mindy	350
Warren	200

Pinball Scores

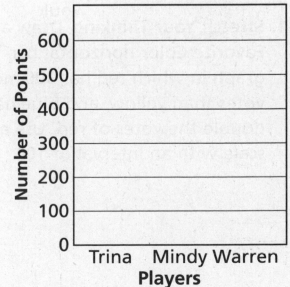

Number of Points

600
500
400
300
200
100
0

Trina   Mindy Warren
Players

Remembering

Multiply or divide to find the unknown numbers.

1. $16 = \underline{\hspace{1cm}} \times 4$

2. $\underline{\hspace{1cm}} = 4 \times 8$

3. $42 \div 7 = \underline{\hspace{1cm}}$

4. $8 = 56 \div \underline{\hspace{1cm}}$

5. $2 \times \underline{\hspace{1cm}} = 10$

6. $9 \times 3 = \underline{\hspace{1cm}}$

Use the horizontal bar graph to answer each question.

7. How many markers are there?

_____

8. How many more crayons are there than pencils?

_____

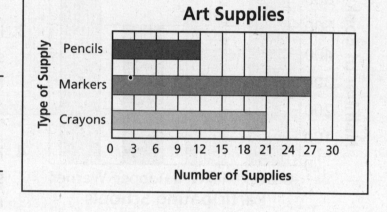

9. How many fewer pencils are there than markers?

_____

10. Write your own question that can be answered using the graph.

_____

_____

11. Stretch Your Thinking Draw a Favorite Color horizontal bar graph in which red has 300 more votes than yellow, and blue has double the votes of red. Use a scale with an interval of 100.

Read and Create Bar Graphs with Multidigit Numbers

Homework

Measure the lengths of 12 shoes at your home to the nearest $\frac{1}{2}$ inch. Record the data in the Tally Chart and then make a Frequency Table.

1.

Tally Chart	
Length	Tally

Frequency Table	
Length	Tally

Use the data above to make a line plot.

2.

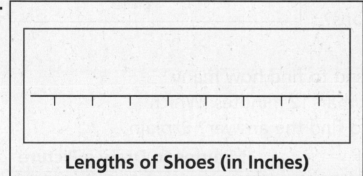

Lengths of Shoes (in Inches)

Use the data displays to answer the questions.

3. What is the length of the shortest shoe? _____

4. What is the length of the longest shoe? _____

5. Which length appears the most often? _____

6. Write a question that can be answered using the data displayed on the line plot.

_____

Name _____ **Date** _____

Remembering

Complete.

1. $9 + (3 \times 0) =$ ☐   **2.** $21 \times 1 =$ ☐   **3.** $4 \times (3 + 3) =$ ☐

4. $3 \times (5 + 1) =$ ☐   **5.** $5 \times 9 = 9 \times$ ☐ $=$ ☐   **6.** $(9 + 1) \times 3 =$ ☐

Use the vertical bar graph to answer the questions.

7. How many more cans did the 3rd grade collect than the 2nd grade? _____

8. How many fewer cans did the 2nd grade collect than the 1st grade? _____

9. About how many more cans would the 4th grade have to collect to have the same number as the grade with the most cans?

_____

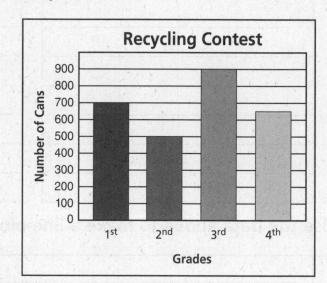

10. Stretch Your Thinking You need to find how many people drew a picture in less than 12 minutes. Which data display is easier to use to find the answer? Explain.

Minutes to Draw Picture			
Steve	10	Rob	14
Lauren	12	Nikki	13
Claudia	14	Jose	15
Erin	15	Tom	15
Joe	13	Helen	11
Greg	15	Tim	14

Minutes to Draw a Picture

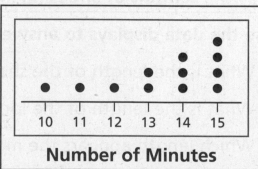

Number of Minutes

_____

_____

Homework

The coach of the girls' soccer team measured the heights of the players to the nearest $\frac{1}{2}$ inch. She recorded the heights in the line plot below.

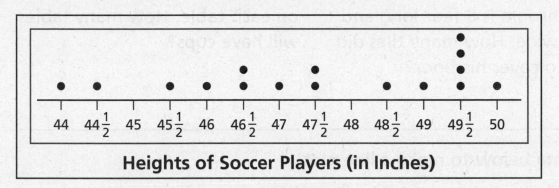

Heights of Soccer Players (in Inches)

Use the line plot to solve the problems.

1. How many players are $47\frac{1}{2}$ inches tall?

_____

2. What is the difference in height between the tallest player on the team and the shortest player?

_____

3. What is the most frequent height?

_____

4. How many players are on the soccer team?

_____

5. Are there more players $47\frac{1}{2}$ inches tall and greater or less than $47\frac{1}{2}$ inches tall?

_____

6. How many more players are $49\frac{1}{2}$ inches than $46\frac{1}{2}$ inches tall?

_____

Remembering

Write an equation and solve the problem.

1. Jon used 1-foot square tiles to cover his bathroom floor. The bathroom is 8 feet long and 10 feet wide. How many tiles did he use to cover his floor?

   _____

2. The principal buys 42 red cups and 21 blue cups. She puts 7 cups on each table. How many tables will have cups?

   _____

Use the data below to make a line plot.

3.

Lengths of Pencils in Inches			
Lizzie	$7\frac{1}{2}$	Carl	6
Mario	5	Aja	6
Jenn	$6\frac{1}{2}$	Joe	$7\frac{1}{2}$
Travis	7	Jung	7
Karen	6	Terrell	7

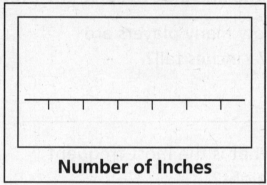

Pencil Lengths

Number of Inches

4. **Stretch Your Thinking** You need to find the height of most third graders at your school. What type of data display would you use? Explain.

   _____

   _____

Homework

Measure the length of a smile of 10 different people to the nearest $\frac{1}{2}$ inch.

1. Record the lengths in the box below.

```
_____

_____

_____

_____

_____

_____

_____

_____

_____

_____
```

2. Organize the measurement data in a frequency table and a line plot.

Frequency Table	
Length	**Tally**

Line Plot

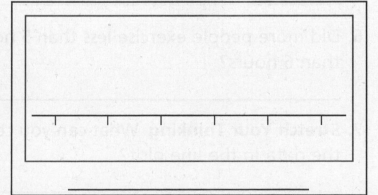

3. Describe what your line plot shows.

_____

_____

Remembering

Write an equation and solve the problem.

1. There are 72 skateboards in the shop. If Todd sells 8 each day, how many days will it take him to sell all of the skateboards?

_____

Complete.

2. 36 = _____ × 4   3. _____ × 9 = 81   4. _____ = 54 ÷ 6

Use the line plot to solve the problems.

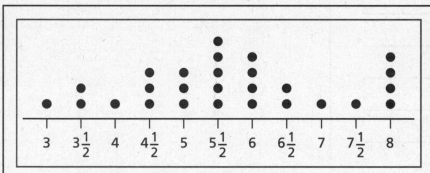

Time in Hours of Exercising for 1 Week

5. How many people exercised for 6 hours?

_____

6. Did more people exercise less than 5 hours or more than 6 hours?

_____

7. **Stretch Your Thinking** What can you conclude about the data in the line plot?

_____

_____